PLUMBING &
CENTRAL HEATING

HAMLYN PRACTICAL DIY GUIDES

PLUMBING &
CENTRAL HEATING

Roger Bisby

HAMLYN

ACKNOWLEDGEMENTS

Technical Consultant:

Mike Trier

●

Editors:

Lizzie Pearl and Lesley McOwan

●

Art Editor:

Pedro Prá Lopez

●

Design:

Michael Leaman

●

Special Photography:

Jon Bouchier

●

Illustration:

Andrew and Simon Green

●

Picture Research:

Emily Hedges

●

Production Controller:

Alyssum Ross

The publishers thank the following companies and organizations for providing the photographs listed below:

Armitage Shanks Bathrooms, Ringley, Staffs; 55, 59 bottom. Aqualisa Products Ltd, Westerham, Kent; 56 bottom. Barking Grohe Ltd, Barking, Essex; 56 top. BC Sanitan, Reading, Berkshire; 55 main pic. British Gas plc; 88. Chaffoteaux Ltd, Redhill, Surrey; 82 bottom. Drayton Controls (Engineering) Ltd, West Drayton, Middlesex; 75. Fernox Mfg Co Ltd, Clavering, Essex; 82 top, 90. Honeywell Control Systems Ltd, Bracknell, Berkshire; 14. Ideal-Standard Ltd, Kingston-Upon-Hull; 53, 54, 59 top, 59 middle. Leisure, Long Eaton, Nottingham; 59 right, 62. Potterton International Ltd, Warwick; 12. Stelrad Ideal; 74 top, 76, 81. Vernon Tutbury; 63. Aqua Ware Ltd; 50.

The Publishers thank the following companies for supplying merchandise for special photography:

IMI Opella; Crangrove.

Subjects for special photography supplied by Sainsburys Homebase.

This edition published in 1990 by
The Hamlyn Publishing Group Limited
a division of
The Octopus Publishing Group
Michelin House
81 Fulham Road
LONDON SW3 6RB

CONTENTS

INTRODUCTION

A constant water supply is undoubtedly one of the greatest luxuries civilisation has to offer. Like so many modern miracles we naturally learn to take it for granted – until something goes wrong.

The first part of this book shows how typical systems work and where you would expect to find the all-important emergency stopcocks. The aim is to take the panic out of the situation and put you back in control.

An early chapter shows how to carry out simple repair and maintenance jobs with a minimal tool kit and recommends a few items no householder should be without.

More involved plumbing projects are then described, with step-by-step instructions on different techniques.

Armed with this information it should be possible for anyone with modest ability to tackle most of the jobs described in the following pages. Naturally, it pays to walk before you run and the absolute beginner should consider smaller jobs first.

PLANNING
The more involved projects such as fitting a new bathroom suite are divided into manageable sections which also show how a great deal of the disruption associated with such jobs can be avoided by careful planning. Many DIY projects grind to a halt, not through lack of enthusiasm or practical ability but because the person carrying out the work has failed to give it sufficient forethought, sometimes including attention to building regulations and water byelaws.

CENTRAL HEATING
Heating systems can cause their own peculiar problems but cannot be considered entirely separately from the plumbing system. The principles and a few emergency repairs are dealt with in the early sections but for anyone wishing to alter or install a complete system the bulk of information is contained in the last section of the book. Notable omissions are system design and connections to the gas pipe. Each is a subject which would take a book in itself and it is recommended that they should be left to a qualified professional.

MANUFACTURERS' INSTRUCTIONS
Variations in design and installation techniques are bound to occur. *To validate guarantees, fitting instructions supplied with any components must take precedence over information given in this book.*

SAFETY
Throughout the book there are references to safety which are intended to form an integral part of the work being described: they are *not* afterthoughts. There is also a chapter on safety with dos and don'ts. Please read them and do not forget them.

THE PLUMBER'S TOOL KIT

Many people assume that successful plumbing can only be achieved with a vast collection of tools. It is true that a plumber's tool kit is among the largest of any tradesman's but most plumbers will readily admit that there are a lot of tools that only get used once in a blue moon. Now that these specialist tools are available for hire and modern fittings have done away with the need for a good many more, the essential tool kit looks far less daunting.

Even so, it is a sizeable investment if all you want to do is change a tap washer, which is why this book has a section on simple plumbing jobs that can be carried out with the tools shown in the emergency kit. This is the basic set of tools no home should be without, unless it has a guaranteed hot line to a 24-hour plumber. Having gained a little confidence carrying out these smaller tasks there is no reason why anyone with even modest ability should not go on to collect a few more tools and tackle some of the larger projects.

THE BASIC KIT

Not all the tools shown below will be needed even for the larger projects. Study the project to find out what is involved. Decide which tools you would be better off hiring. Some tools such as the jigsaw and hand saw might perform many of the same tasks; however, if you are cutting a hole in a worktop, for example, the jigsaw, although indispensable, might only be worth hiring.

- Pipe cutters for copper
- Junior hacksaw for cutting pipes *in situ*
- Claw hammer
- Flat-bladed screwdriver (medium)
- Flat-bladed screwdriver (small)
- Electrical neon test screwdriver
- Pozidriv screwdriver (medium)
- Pozidriv screwdriver (small)
- Adjustable grips
- Stillsons (can be hired)
- Club hammer
- Blowlamp
- Heat-resistant mat

- Steel tape
- Flat file (small)
- Electric drill
- Masonry bits
- Hole saw (multibladed)
- Electric jigsaw
- General purpose hand saw
- Open-ended adjustable spanner
- Bending springs (15mm and 22mm)
- Spirit level (small)
- Sink plunger
- Combination pliers
- Crowsfoot basin spanner
- Radiator valve key

Right: 1: Tap tool 2: Mole wrench. 3: pliers. 4: claw hammer. 5: club hammer. 6: sink plunger. 7: brick bolster. 8: cold chisel. 9: adjustable spanner. 10: pipe wrench. 11: junior hacksaw. 12: hacksaw. 13: spirit level. 14: extension lead. 15: general-purpose saw. 16: flat file. 17: blowlamp and heat-resistant mat. 18: tape measure. 19: jig saw. 20: pipe cutter. 21: secateurs for plastic pipe. 22: pipe snake. 23: immersion heater spanner. 24 & 25: pipe bending springs. 26: drill, hole saws and bits. 27: radiator valve keys. 28: sink plunger. 29: screwdriver with interchangeable bits.

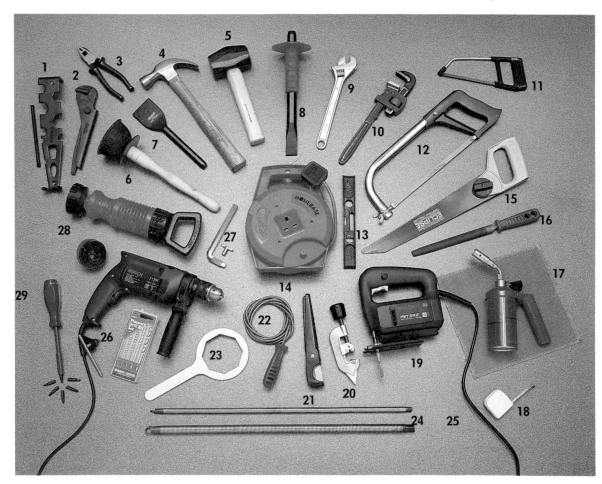

ACCESSORIES

PTFE (Polytetrafluoroethylene) tape A non-sticky tape used for sealing threaded joints.

Boss Blue A sealing compound which is approved for use on drinking water supplies. It is not always necessary but is a useful stand-by for troublesome joints.

Lead-free solder This is used for end-feed fittings. Solder ring fittings have the solder in them and do not require extra.

Flux A paste used to help solder run easily around a joint when it is heated with a blowlamp.

Steel wool Used to polish copper pipe before it is soldered.

Silicone sealant (Fernox XLS) This can be used for sealing pressure joints and a variety of emergency repairs.

Silicone lubricant Used on push-fit rubber seals.

HIRE TOOLS

The range of tools offered for hire is constantly expanding, so it is always worth checking to see what is available. Listed here are some of the tools which make plumbing projects easier.

If you have never used a particular tool before, make sure you are really certain about how it works. This is particularly important with power tools that may be more powerful than anything you are used to. Always use recommended safety equipment such as eye protection and a dust mask.

Pipe benders The hand-held model bends 15-mm and 22-mm pipe only.

Immersion heater spanner For removing or fitting immersions into cylinders. Do not ever use wrenches for this.

Drain-unblocking equipment.

Electric rotary hammer This can be used as a breaker or, by changing the bit, can be turned into a powerful hammer drill.

Core bit For cutting neat large-diameter holes (up to 150-mm [6-in]) through brick, and must be used with the electric rotary hammer.

Blowlamp For soldering.

Above: 1: *Soldier and flux.* **2:** *plumber's putty.* **3:** *sealing compound.* **4:** *PTFE tape.* **5:** *pipe freezing kit.* **6:** *wire wool.* **7:** *bath sealant and cartridge gun.*

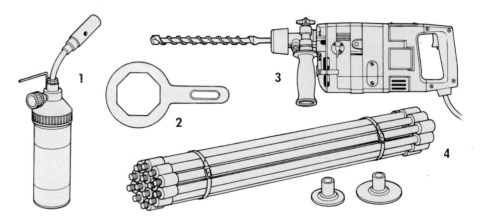

Above: 1: *Blow lamp* **2:** *Immersion heater spanner* **3:** *Electric rotary hammer* **4:** *Drain-cleaning rods and rod ends.*

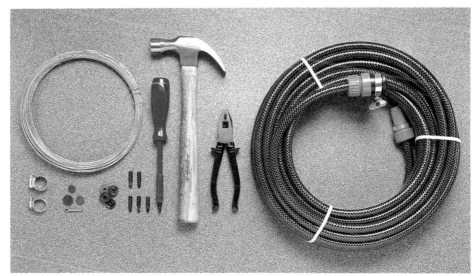

Above: *If a plumbing emergency does happen, having a few tools and accessories to hand makes all the difference.*

EMERGENCY KIT

- Pipe repair kit
- Hammer
- Screwdriver with selection of blades
- Tap and ballvalve washers
- Combination pliers
- PTFE tape
- Garden hose
- Length of wire
- Piece of rubber (old hot water bottle)

HOW WATER REACHES YOUR TAPS

The pipes that crisscross the average house are often a mystery to the owner. If something goes wrong, the unfortunate owner is in the front line. Knowing what, where and how to turn off is something everyone in the home should know, yet surveys suggest that many people do not know where their main stopcock is. Even if this is the only thing you learn about plumbing, find out today.

If you do not end up tackling any major projects, having some idea of what is involved is a good way to make sure a disreputable tradesman cannot make a relatively simple job seem like a complicated (more expensive) one. The following few pages take a look at some of the traditional plumbing and heating systems found in houses and flats. There are also some more recent developments finding their way into new homes which look set to become the standard plumbing systems of the future.

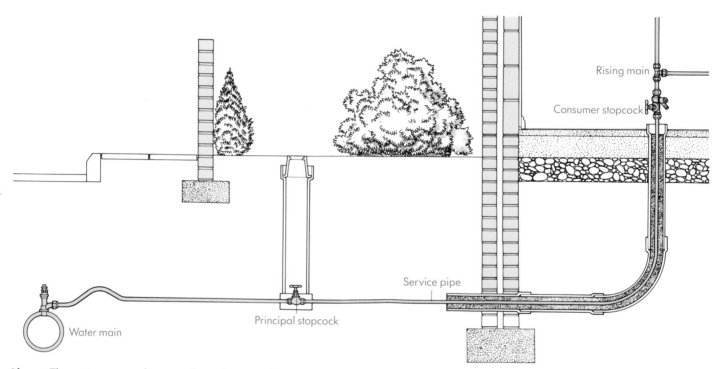

Above: The route your underground supply pipe takes as it runs from the main under the road to your rising main stop tap.

YOUR UNDERGROUND PIPE

The underground service pipe brings water from the main in the road to your home. The short section of communication pipe from the road main to the water suppliers' own underground stopcock on or near your boundary is their responsibility. From that point on the pipe belongs to the property owner. Any leaks that occur on this section can be repaired by the owner but **must** be inspected by the water authority.

Older underground pipes were made of lead, galvanized iron or copper. All are liable to corrode.

Modern service pipe is made of blue plastic, called Medium Density Polyethylene (MDPE). It can be used to replace sections of old pipe or to renew the complete length. Adaptors are available to join any type of pipe to polyethylene.

In some soft water areas, where lead pipe is considered to be a health hazard, grants may be available to help with the cost of renewal.

The pipe should be laid at a depth of 750mm (30 in), but in some older properties pipes were laid as shallow as 300mm (12 in); so you may come across the service pipe when digging.

Normally, pipes are laid in a straight line between the outside (principal) stopcock and the internal (consumer) stopcock. If you are unsure about the exact location of the pipe, ask your local water authority.

Leaks

Suspect a leak on the underground pipe if you hear a rushing noise on the internal plumbing when no water is being used. The water authority will test the pipe.

The service pipe enters the building through the foundations and comes up through the floor to a stopcock. This is the point for controlling the water supply into the house. It is the most important emergency shut-off point and should always be accessible. Test it from time to time, as infrequent use makes it stiff.

If the stopcock does not turn off totally it will need rewashering.

TANK-FED SYSTEM

Right: Where to turn off: The stopcock controls all incoming water. Gate valves control water from the tank to the cylinder and taps. To turn off the hot taps, close the gate valve on the supply to the cylinder. Washing machine taps are connected to flexible hoses.

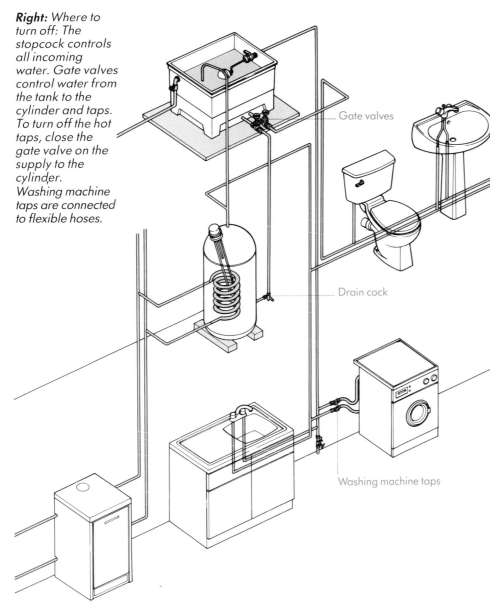

Gate valves

Drain cock

Washing machine taps

Water pressure at the taps is governed by the height of the cold water tank. This is known as the 'head' and is a critical factor when considering installing a shower. If space allows, the tank can be raised up on a strong wooden platform inside the loft. The condition and size of pipes will also affect the flow. If the pipes are badly scaled or corroded, the effective bore could be dramatically reduced. Airlocks or spluttering can result if the cylinder is not replenished fast enough by the feed from the cold tank, possibly due to scale.

How it works

This design, officially known as the indirect system, is the most common in the UK. Only the kitchen drinking water, and perhaps a washing machine, are supplied from the mains. Everything else is fed by a large storage tank.

The water going into the tank is controlled by a ballvalve which shuts off the supply when the level is high enough. The tank, being higher than the plumbing outlets, provides a constant pressure (head) for the taps and wc cistern.

The cold taps and wc cistern are fed directly from the tank, usually by a single pipe with branches.

The hot taps are fed via a copper cylinder which may be heated by a boiler or electric immersion heater.

The cold water enters the cylinder at the bottom and, because it is fed by the higher tank, maintains a constant pressure in the cylinder. As the water is heated it rises inside the cylinder, so the hottest water is always at the top. A feature of this system is the cylinder vent, which must remain open to act as an escape route for air and overheated water.

The fact that water finds its own level is used to advantage in this system. Usually, the water in the vent pipe will rise and fall with the water in the storage tank. It is only when a thermostat fails that the water in the vent pipe rises over the top and gushes into the tank. If this happens, the water heater must be turned off immediately. Do not close any valves.

Hot taps can be run which will cool things down.

Loft pipes must not freeze. A frozen vent and cold feed can cause a cylinder to collapse or explode.

MAINS-FED, NO STORAGE

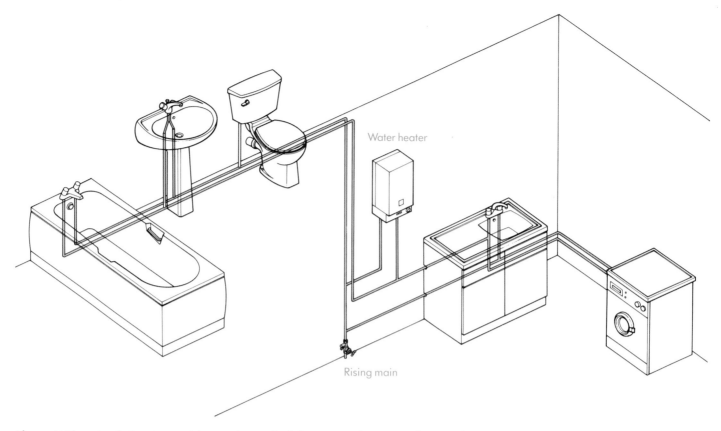

Above: With mains-fed systems cold water is supplied direct to appliances and to a multi-point water heater.

The mains-fed system is often used in flats, where no stored water can be accommodated. The incoming water is controlled by the consumer stopcock which shuts off both the hot and cold water for the flats.

All cold taps, washing machine, WC and cold supply to the shower are fed directly from the mains. Individual isolating valves should be incorporated for servicing appliances without having to shut off the water to the rest of the house.

The hot water is supplied through a gas-fired multipoint instantaneous water heater or, more recently, possibly an unvented cylinder (see page 15). Sometimes, pressure-balancing valves are fitted to stabilize the flow between hot and cold taps.

The shower should contain its own flow stabilizers. A non-return valve (double-check valve) must be fitted on a flexible shower hose if there is the possibility of the shower head being under water. This is to prevent contaminating the mains drinking water through back siphonage.

Advantages of having no storage:

- Economical hot water – you pay only for what is used.
- Constant supply of hot water.
- Space-saving and quick to install.
- Good shower pressure.
- All pipework is within the building – little risk of frost damage.
- One position emergency shut-off point.

Disadvantages of no storage:

- No stored water in case of mains failure.
- Unsuitable for low-pressure mains water, such as a single shared supply to several homes.
- No back-up heater.
- Takes longer to run a bath.
- Hot water pressures can be erratic, even non existent, when other taps are being used.

Right: Modern gas-fired wall-mounted boilers combine big outputs with small sizes.

THE COMBINATION BOILER

A combination boiler provides central heating and instant hot water within one gas-fired unit. For small homes, this boiler is a good option.

The flow is switched from the central heating to the hot water when a tap is turned on, and returns when no more hot water is required.

HEATING

How it works

Heating system designs vary from the one shown below, but the principles are very similar. More information on the components and controls is given in the heating section of this book but, as heating and hot water plumbing are integrated, it is worth considering the system as a whole rather than separate parts.

A modern central heating system uses a single boiler to provide hot water through the cylinder coil and heating through the radiators. The basic idea is to divert water from the boiler to the radiators and/or the cylinder as required. In this system the hot water reaches the cylinder by gravity circulation. Cold water, being heavier, pushes the hot water out through the primary flow from the boiler. It passes through the cylinder inside a sealed copper coil heat exchanger to prevent it mixing with the tap water stored inside. The

cool water returns to the boiler, pushing more hot water out as it goes.

As the cylinder water reaches the desired temperature selected on the boiler thermostat, the returning water will be the same temperature as the flow and circulation will cease naturally. The cylinder thermostat will switch off the boiler or leave it to supply the radiators only.

The radiator flow and return is forced round by an electric pump which is controlled by a room thermostat wired to the main programmer. Individual radiators can be turned on and off by the handvalve or by automatic thermostatic radiator valves (see page 75).

On this system there is a towel rail fed from the gravity hot water circuit. This is independent of the heating circuit and provides a gentle heat. It can be controlled by a manual or thermostatic valve, unless the boiler is fired by solid fuel – in which

case the towel rail must remain on as an escape for excess heat.

The water in the boiler and its circuits is supplied from a feed and expansion tank well above the highest radiator. Once the system is filled, the tank tops up water lost by evaporation. It also provides a reservoir to hold water displaced by natural expansion when the boiler heats up the system. As a result, the water level will rise and fall slightly as the boiler operates. If water discharges from the vent pipe it means that the boiler thermostat is faulty or the system is badly designed.

Below: *The heating system. To drain it:*
1 *Turn off the boiler and electrical supply to the controls. Allow the water to cool.*
2 *Tie up the ballvalve float arm*
in the feed and expansion tank to prevent it dropping.
3 *Attach a hosepipe to the drain-off pipe and run it out to an outside drain, then open the draincock two turns.*

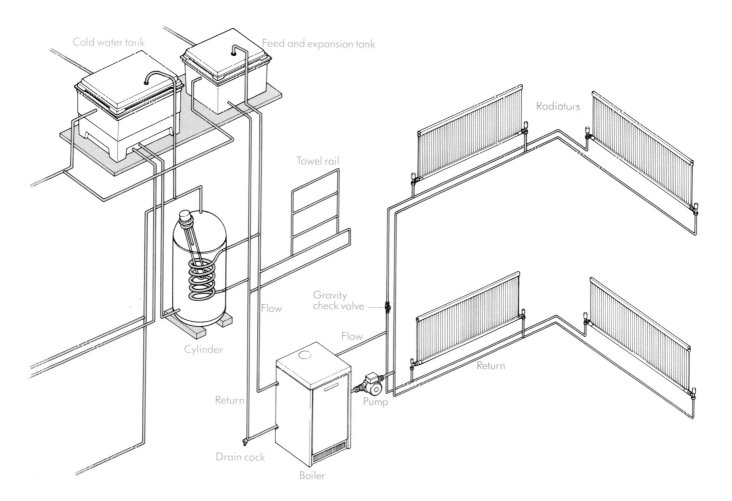

Cold water tank
Feed and expansion tank
Radiators
Towel rail
Flow
Gravity check valve
Flow
Cylinder
Return
Return
Pump
Drain cock
Boiler

FULLY-PUMPED HEATING AND WATER

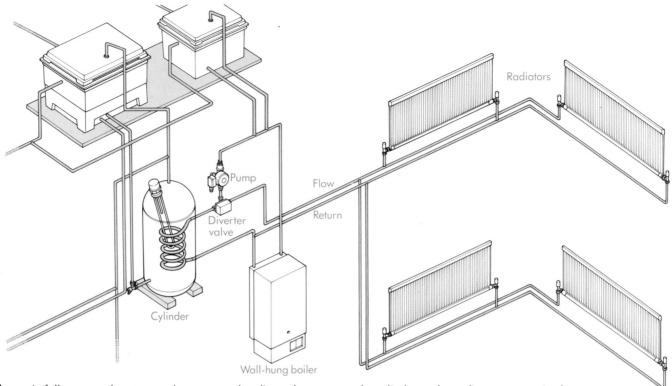

Above: In fully-pumped systems, a three-way valve diverts hot water to the cylinder or the radiators as required.

The fully-pumped system uses a pump to take water from the boiler around the hot water and radiator circuits. This gives a faster heat-up time for the cylinder and greater economy. It is therefore the ideal system for a large household where hot water demand is likely to be high over short periods in the mornings when the household is preparing for school or work, and in the evenings on their return.

With no dependence upon natural gravity forces to move the water around the circuits, the boiler can be mounted anywhere in relation to the cylinder and, in most cases, nothing larger than 22-mm pipework will be needed to connect the two. This is a great advantage if the boiler needs to be one side of the house and the cylinder the other.

Space-saving gas wall-hung boilers are a popular choice for this type of system, but any type of boiler except solid fuel can be used. There must be a clear path from the boiler to the open vent as well as a permanent route to the boiler from the feed and expansion tank.

The controls

The heating and hot water circuits are controlled by the master programmer, which has a time-clock. Each circuit also has a thermostat for temperature control.

The controls are connected to a motorized valve, or valves, which direct the water from the boiler to

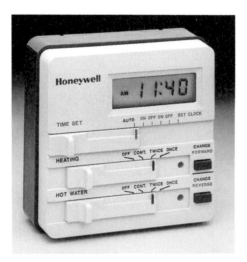

Above: A modern, electronic programmer with digital timer can be programmed to give spot-on accuracy of timing.

where it is needed. The two-way valve will serve both circuits or only one. It can be wired to give priority to a particular circuit, which is useful if the boiler is working near to full capacity. This allows the boiler to be switched to heating the hot water cylinder only, rather than letting it struggle for hours trying to serve both circuits. The drawback is that the radiators will go cold for, perhaps, 30 minutes.

The other control type is the zone valve, which opens and closes a particular circuit. A pair of zone valves can perform the same function as a diverter valve but as they are separate there is freedom of system design and pipe layout.

The zone valves can be wired to be controlled separately if desired, and to be operated manually, by thermostat, or by timeswitch or programmer, enabling the system to be designed for both practicality and economy.

HIGH-PRESSURE HOT WATER

Unvented hot water systems have been used abroad for many years but it is only relatively recently that they have been legal in the UK.

The cold supply comes directly from the mains – thereby overcoming the need for tanks in the roof space, which can be a source of bursts in the winter. Provided there is sufficient mains pressure, a powerful shower can be had from this type of system, in contrast to the inadequate drizzle which is so often a feature of tank-fed plumbing.

Unvented systems are fitted with a number of safety devices which are required in Britain to meet very stringent safety requirements. Specialist knowledge and equipment is required to install and maintain these systems and this must be left to a qualified professional. Once installed and checked by the Building Control Officer at the town hall, the plumbing on the outlet side can be carried out by a DIYer as with any other hot water system. In most cases, the pipes can be kept as small as 15-mm rather than the more expensive 22-mm.

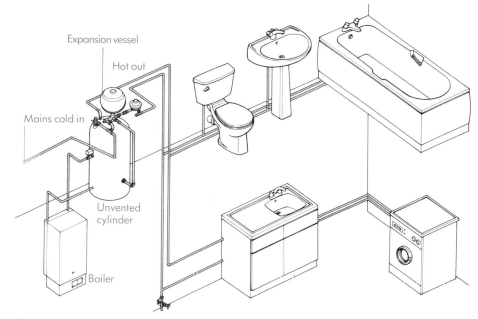

Above: In modern unvented hot water systems, an expansion vessel and mains top-up facility eliminates the need for a header tank.

UK bath taps

Generally, British taps have low-pressure outlets, which might cause a great deal of steam if used on high-pressure hot water systems. The flow can be reduced by a valve on the supply pipe to the taps.

THERMAL STORE

An alternative to the unvented system is the thermal store cylinder, which gives the advantages of high-pressure hot water without the stringent regulations. This means it can be installed by a DIY plumber and does not require pressure valves or an overflow. Like the unvented system, it is dependent upon a good incoming mains pressure but as it is not normally fitted with a flow pressure regulator there could be fluctuations when other taps are used.

How it works

The water in the cylinder remains captive inside the boiler circuit, acting only as a way of transferring heat from the boiler to the cylinder.

The water that supplies the hot taps comes from the rising main and, rather than being stored, passes through the cylinder as a hot tap is run. The rapid heat transfer from the stored water to the flowing water is made possible by a high-efficiency copper heat-exchanger coil. A thermostatic mixing valve is often fitted to keep the water temperature constant at the taps. This allows the water in the cylinder to be kept hot, making it suitable for radiators.

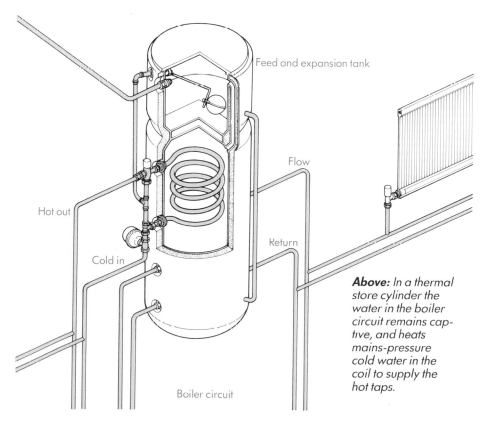

Above: In a thermal store cylinder the water in the boiler circuit remains captive, and heats mains-pressure cold water in the coil to supply the hot taps.

HOW WATER LEAVES YOUR HOME

Modern plastic waste and drainage components are reputed to be 'child's play' to assemble, but there is more to drainage than putting together fittings. The design and installation is governed by the building by-laws, which in this respect are concerned with safeguarding health. Any addition or alteration must be approved by the Building Control Officer at the town hall, who will also advise on permissible variations.

Underground blockages

These can be cleared by lifting the manhole covers and plunging with drain rods. If the blockage is beyond the last manhole, consult your local council. Rainwater drains vary, depending on local conditions. In some areas a rainwater drain system is used to take water from gutters; in others rainwater runs to a soakaway in the garden. No house water should be discharged into rainwater gulleys as it can pollute rivers.

Above ground

The single stack system is now the legal requirement for new installations. The vital parts of any waste system are the traps, or 'U' bends. These are water seals, or barriers, against smells and germs coming from the drains. Each fitment has its own trap at the head of the pipe run. The wc is the only fitment that has a built-in trap. The soil stack has all the foul water connections made separately to avoid siphonage of the trap seal, which can lead to smells.

The wc is connected to a 100-mm (4-in) branch with a gradual fall to the vertical soil and vent pipe. Upstairs, the soil pipe must run to a vertical open vent to stop suction pulling the trap water out. The top of the vent must be above the gutter and clear of windows to stop smells entering. Downstairs the wc is usually connected directly to the drains.

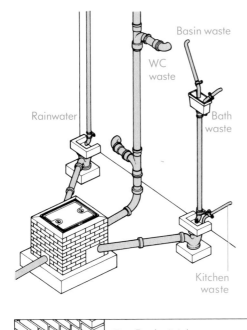

Rainwater
Basin waste
WC waste
Bath waste
Kitchen waste

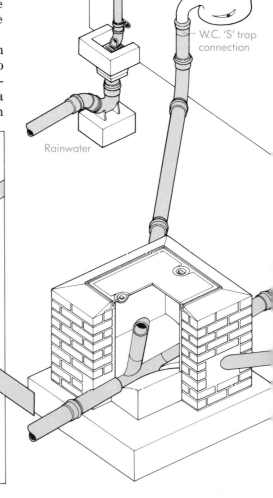

W.C. 'S' trap connection

Rainwater

Fresh air inlet

Manhole

Interceptor trap

Basin wastes These are connected to a 32-mm (1¼-in) bottle or tubular trap (see page 38), depending upon which is neatest and fits more easily.

The 32-mm (1¼-in) waste-pipe should be sloped at a gentle gradient of approximately 1 in 30. Any run steeper or longer than 1.5m (5ft) should have an anti-siphon trap fitted, or an increased pipe diameter over some of its final length to prevent it running full.

tray. As connections to a soil stack must have the protection of a 75-mm (3-in) trap, low-level traps can only legally be discharged into open gullies. If space is tight and the fitment cannot be raised, a running trap can be fitted in the pipe line.

Ventilating the drains The open top of the vent pipe should be fitted with a wire or plastic guard to stop birds nesting in it. This pipe which releases smells, particularly during the summer, is often referred to as

pipe might have to be extended.

Ground floor Appliances often go to an outside gully to keep them independent of the soil stack. The washing machine, dishwasher and sink are discharged into 40-mm (1½-in) waste-pipes protected by a trap(s). Sink traps with washing machine spigots provide a neat and simple means of connecting everything into one pipe without risk of siphonage, and with the advantage that hot water and detergents from the machines keep the waste free of grease and smells. If a waste disposal unit is fitted, the waste-pipe discharges below the gully grid.

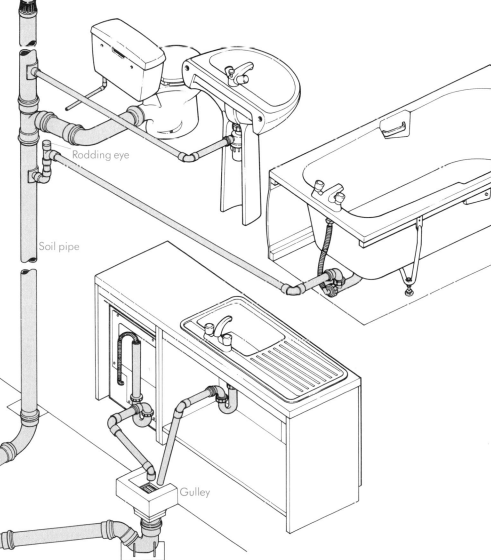

Rodding eye

Soil pipe

Gulley

Left: A well designed waste system will run smoothly with minimal noise. Straight pipe runs make blockages unlikely, and deep traps keep smells out of the home.

Waste disposal units

Waste disposal units grind up small scraps by flinging them against cutters in a centrifuge. The process works best with plenty of water running through the unit so leave the tap running. If the unit overheats a manual reset button on the bottom should be pushed in.

Centrifugal cutters

Motor

Plug

Above: *Waste disposal units can be fitted to most modern sinks.*

Bath and shower wastes Mostly, these are 40mm (1½in) in diameter but are available in different depths to cope with the problem of limited space under a low bath or shower

the stink pipe. It must be positioned at least 900mm (3ft) above or away from windows within 3 metres (10ft). Where a dormer window or skylight is added to a house the vent

SAFETY

There will be those readers who, at the very sight of the word safety, will skip to another page. It is easy to understand their desire to get on with the real job immediately. Nobody wants to waste time with unproductive distractions when there is something to get done. After all, they can always return to this section later, when they have finished what they want to do or when the odd spare moment arises.

SAFETY = QUALITY

The belief that safety is time-consuming and unproductive is a myth that stems from the attitude that everything is achieved by charging head-on at maximum speed. In fact, the safe job is invariably better, often quicker and always more pleasurable.

Most safety is commonsense. There will be few revelations on these pages but, with any luck, many reminders.

Ladders Work from a quick tower if possible. Tie ladders to screw-eyes at the top. Avoid resting the ladder on a gutter where it might slip sideways. Avoid uneven or soft ground unless it is possible to bury the feet. Get a helper to steady the ladder at the bottom. Pitch ladders at 1 unit out to 4 units up. Check ladders are in good order.

Towers Tie the tower or use outrigger stabilizing struts. Climb the inside, preferably on a purpose-made stairway. Use safety rails and toe boards to stop tools being kicked over the edge.

CHILDREN AND SAFETY

Children are drawn towards work areas because they are interesting. They do not know the difference between a live wire and a dead one.
- Lock tools away.
- Cover over work areas.
- Remove ladders when not working. When you are working, do not let children play below.

The odd spare moment may arise sooner than expected. By then it may be too late. Accidents are always like that. One minute you are rushing along trying to get the job done, even seconds are valuable, then suddenly it all stops dead. It was perhaps the difference between fetching a pair of goggles from the shed or getting on with cutting that hole in the wall. Often that is all it boils down to, just a few seconds.

Only go on a roof if you are confident of your ability to work safely. It is no saving over using a professional if you end up injuring yourself. Ridge-hook roof ladders and chimney scaffolds should be used for jobs such as lining the flue, if not a full scaffold. If the roof is tiled it is often possible to slip a few tiles out to give an extra fixing point around the battens for ridge ladders. The golden rule on roofs is "Double up for safety". This means never relying on one fixing point, it might let you down (literally!).

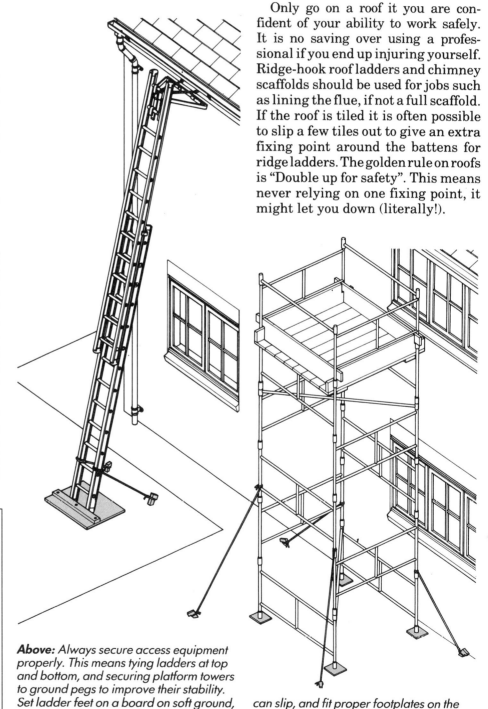

Above: Always secure access equipment properly. This means tying ladders at top and bottom, and securing platform towers to ground pegs to improve their stability. Set ladder feet on a board on soft ground, pegged so that neither board nor ladder can slip, and fit proper footplates on the lowest frames of platform towers.

Electricity Turn off the power when working on circuits. Check flexes on power tools etc are not damaged.

Never join wires with insulating tape; use in-line connectors for flexes; use junction boxes for cable. Always install the correct fuse rating in amps:

$Watts \div volts = amps$

- Never leave extension leads or power tools plugged in, especially in bathrooms where there is water.
- Use an RCD circuit-breaker on power tools and any type of outdoor supply.

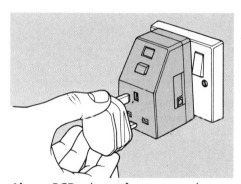

Above: RCD adaptor for power tools.

Power tools Use power tools only for their proper purpose; never remove guards.
- Wear eye protection to guard against flying debris.
- Keep hands away from cutting edges.
- Keep hair away from drill bits.
- Do not wear loose clothing which might catch in revolving parts.

Above: Wear goggles to drill masonry.

Breathing and eye protection Avoid inhaling chemical fumes.
- Wear a dust mask whenever there is a danger from polluted air, visible or not.
- Ventilate confined spaces when working with hazardous materials. Take care with asbestos; if in doubt, seek advice.
- Always use goggles or safety glasses when drilling, chiselling or high-speed cutting.

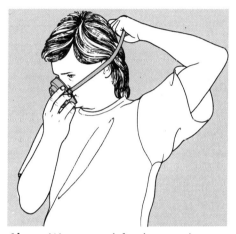

Above: Wear a mask for dusty work.

Fire Take care with blowlamps. Do not leave a naked flame burning whilst unattended. Check the area at intervals after use.
- Keep a fire extinguisher handy.
- Do not burn plastics or other materials liable to give off toxic gases.
- Fit a smoke alarm.

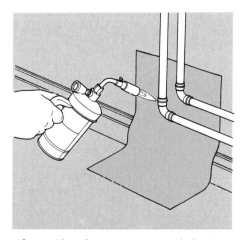

Above: Place heat-resistant mat behind capillary fittings when you solder them.

Gas Always use a professional for work on gas pipes, and have appliances serviced and checked for leaks and malfunctions.

Ventilate open (conventional) flue appliances such as boilers. Do not adapt or alter gas-fired appliances.

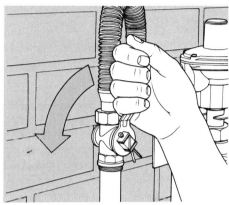

Above: Always ensure that the gas supply is turned off at the mains before working on gas supply pipes and appliances.

FIRST AID
In the case of anything other than minor accidents, see a doctor.
Burns and scalds Minor injuries must be held under cold water until the pain eases, after which a light sterile dressing can be applied. Do not use cream or lotion without medical advice. If the burn appears serious or the skin is badly broken then see a doctor.
Electric shock The risk of serious injury is worse where water is involved. If the victim is still in contact with the current, try to separate them from the current using a non-conductive object – a wooden broom for instance – or switch the current off. Do not touch them until this is done. Call an ambulance if the victim is unconscious. Give artificial respiration if you can.
Eye injuries Dust or grit in the eye can often be washed out by bathing the eye in cold water and blinking. Do not rub the eye. Splashes of chemicals must be washed with running water.

SPOTTING EMERGENCIES

Many plumbing emergencies can be avoided by recognizing the tell-tale signs early on and acting upon them. Plumbing problems rarely cure themselves. A dripping overflow may have a day off but it will be back with a vengeance the next day.

The checks here are described as seasonal but all plumbing problems should be dealt with as they arise, though at certain times they become more urgent. For example, in the winter a frozen overflow drip can cause the tank to flood the house; and in the summer, lack of use in a heating system can store up trouble and present you with an unwelcome bill right at the start of the winter.

WINTER

Overflows in tanks and WC cisterns The water level should rest at least 25mm (1in) below the outlet. On mains-pressure ballvalves the level is likely to rise at night, forcing water through, so look for wet patches on the ground first thing in the morning. To remedy this, rewasher or renew (see page 26).

severe; a pipe that is not used, such as the cold supply to the feed and expansion tank ballvalve, is in danger (see page 92).

Below: At night, increased mains pressure can cause a worn ballvalve to leak. Since no water is being drawn off, the water level rises and can eventually reach the overflow pipe. Cure the problem by rewashering or replacing the valve, or by reducing the water pressure.

Central heating Set a time-clock to come on at night when temperatures are coldest, or to tick over for 24 hours. Many central heating thermostats have a frost setting which will enable you to leave the heating on permanently at very little cost.

Even with the mains turned off, the central heating will work. With heat going through the pipes and the system on the move there is less chance of a burst pipe on the heating circuit. Other circuits will also benefit.

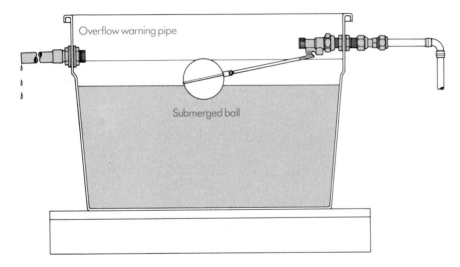

Overflow warning pipe

Submerged ball

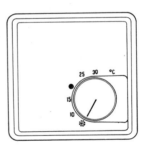

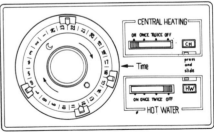

Above: If the house is empty in the winter, turn thermostats down and set the programmer to tick over 24 hours a day.

Outside tap Turn off the outside tap isolating valve. If you have not got an isolating valve, consider fitting one before the bad weather (see page 69).

Stopcocks The stopcock is your first line of defence. Check that it works. Make sure everyone knows where it is and mark on the wall or cupboard which way is off. If it does not work, rewasher it (see page 27).

Insulation Check all pipe and tank insulation is still intact. Has any been removed for maintenance and not put back? It only takes one small section to be left uncovered to cause problems. Frequently used pipes do not freeze unless the conditions are

GOING AWAY

Leaving the house unoccupied during the winter is a worry for many people. There are those who like to turn everything off, including the gas, and those who like to leave it all going. If specific instructions are given by your insurance company, follow them; after all, it is ultimately their loss.

Turn off the mains water This will at least stop a burst pipe pouring water through the building for days.

If there is a risk of the cold water tank freezing, you can drain it by turning on the bath taps. Leave the water in the small tank.

CENTRAL HEATING ANTIFREEZE

If you prefer to turn the gas off while you are away, the heating system can be treated with special central heating antifreeze to give added protection against frosts. It can then be left switched off.

SUMMER CHECKS

Summer checks are largely confined to the central heating system. With any luck, this is the time to forget heating, which is just what most people do.

Boiler service The rush to get boilers serviced and little problems sorted out on the system as soon as the first cold snap comes is evidence of this seasonal neglect. If you can remember to have the boiler serviced in the summer you will be able to choose which day the engineer comes and probably also receive better attention.

Running the system Components such as the valves and pump are liable to stick if left in the same position for too long. The result is that when the heating is switched back on for the first time, the electric motor burns out.

To guard against this, run the system (with the boiler off, if you prefer) for 10 minutes every fortnight or so. Put it through a number of switching cycles to help move the water around and free the valves and pump bearings.

Radiator valves Check valves for leaks around the packing gland which will cause a drip down around the pipe. This is often dried up by the heat in the winter, but in the summer it can cause a damp patch on the ceiling or rotting carpets around the pipe. (See taps, page 25.)

Feed and expansion tank Check for evaporation in the central heating feed and expansion tank in the loft. Often, the ballvalve sticks in the closed position and the water evaporates out. There should only be 75-100mm (3-4in) in the bottom when the system is cold.

If the ballvalve is jammed do not just free it, because it will probably jam in the open position. Take it apart and clean the scale off the brass parts to make sure it operates freely and rewasher it at the same time.

Replace the cover and insulation on the tank – it helps cut down evaporation.

Sludge and scale A well-installed heating system should not suffer from these problems and once filled there is no need for draining at all. In fact, to do so will increase the chances of corrosion but if your heating system is suffering from the effects of sludge or scale, giving it cold spots and making it sluggish, summer is the time to do something about it. Draining down and flushing through a system will help remove sludge but for a thorough job it is best to descale it and remove each radiator in order to take it outside and hose it through with clean running water. Descaling fluids are available for heating and water circuits and more information is given about these on page 89.

(See taps, page 25.)

THERMOSTATIC RADIATOR VALVES

Thermostatic radiator valves are a particular problem in the summer. During prolonged periods in one position some valves are liable to seize in the closed position. The valves should be left on their highest setting so they are at least opening and closing during the night, even if only slightly.

Gutters and downpipes Summer is also a good time to check gutters and downpipes, because you will feel more inclined to make the necessary repairs or renewals.

Use a ladder to examine them carefully. Remove debris from inside with a small trowel.

Leaking joints can be cleaned up and resealed with gunnable mastic specially made for the job. If the gutters are in very bad condition they should be replaced before they fall and cause damage or injury. Lightweight plastic gutters are easy to fit. The hardest part of the job will probably be removing the old gutters safely. See the advice on page 18 about working safely at heights.

Drains. Check all gullys and drains to ensure the water is getting away properly. Blocked drains can be rodded or plunged with a disc plunger.

Left: Check radiator valves for leaks round the spindle, which can cause damp patches on floorcoverings in summer. Tighten the gland nut slightly, or repack the gland if this does not work.

DEALING WITH EMERGENCIES

It is an easy thing to say, 'Don't panic'; but when water is pouring through the ceiling, panicking seems an appropriate course of action to take – often resulting in a frantic telephone call to one of the vast army who gather under the heading of '24-hour emergency plumbers'. Not that it is always easy to get someone to come out immediately. As that little Dutch boy who held his finger in the dam discovered, it can be a long night.

Mercifully, not all emergencies are so dramatic. The fault-finding chart below contains some of the more common faults that occur in plumbing and heating systems. The chart is not exhaustive, and you may end up having to call in a specialist after all. Even if you only manage to get through the weekend with an emergency repair, the difference in call-out charges between Sunday and Monday will make it worthwhile.

FAULT-FINDING CHART

SYMPTOM	POSSIBLE CAUSE	CURE
Running tap	split washer	new washer
Overflow pipe dripping	faulty ballvalve	new washer or seating
No water at hot taps	air lock dry tank, grit in ballvalve	blow out dismantle valve
No water at cold tap in kitchen	mains fault	check with neighbours; contact water authority
No water at cold taps in bathroom	air lock, blocked ballvalve	blow out dismantle valve
No hot water (cold)	boiler out motorized valve stuck pump jammed immersion heater burnt out	relight use manual lever use manual restart replace
Noise in pipes (mains)	pressure too high	turn down, check ballvalve
Leaking radiator valve	worn gland packing	repack gland
Leaking radiator	corrosion hole	turn off valves; replace radiator
Cold radiator	air in top	bleed with key through the top vent screw
WC does not empty	blockage	rod through or plunge
WC won't flush	faulty mechanism or diaphragm	remove plunger and replace diaphragm
Waste-pipe gurgling	blockage developing	plunge or chemically clean
Boiler making noises, kettling or banging	scale	descale
Boiler sending hot water through vent pipe	thermostat	replace thermostat

EMERGENCY REPAIRS

Stopping the flow

The conventional ways of stopping water flowing through pipes are shown in the illustration, but stopcocks and gate valves are notorious for not working when you want them to. If they do not work, here are some alternative ways of stopping the water.

When a tank-fed supply will not turn off because of a faulty gate valve:

1 Use a bottle cork in the cold tank outlet to stop the water.
2 Drain the tank through the taps and turn off the cold supply at the main stopcock.
3 If you need to empty a tank because a gate valve has jammed closed and cannot be replaced with the water in the tank, use a hosepipe to siphon it out.
4 If you cannot turn off a supply to a ballvalve, tie up the arm by placing a piece of timber over the tank and tying the string to it, or hammering a nail in a rafter and tying to that.
5 If an indoor stopcock will not stop the water, turn off the one in the garden. If you do not have a key, you can make one from a stout length of timber, cutting a vee notch in one

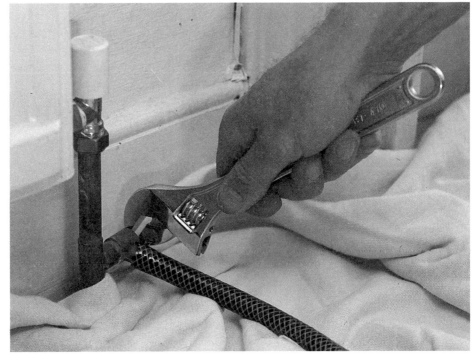

Above: Fit hosepipe to a drain cock and open the valve with an adjustable spanner.

end for tap-head stopcocks.
6 For square-headed stopcocks, use a piece of steel pipe made slightly oval at the end to squeeze over the spigot.
7 As a last alternative, if you cannot get the local water authority emergency service to attend, dig

around the stopcock pit until you have access to the side of the valve, then use a pair of grips.

Using a pipe-freezing kit

Pipe-freezing kits are useful for stopping the water if there is no other way. If you use them for routine jobs, such as renewing radiator valves, make sure you have everything ready to hand.

For emergency work Flatten the pipe with a hammer or stop the flow with a push-fit cap. Wrap the freezer muff around the pipe and insert the nozzle into the muff. Make sure there are no gaps at the top and bottom for the freezant to escape. Protect the fingers from the top – the chemical burns.

Give the recommended number of squirts. There is no point in over-injecting, because the pipe can only absorb at a certain rate.

Wait several minutes until you hear the ice forming inside the pipe, then very gently release the stop end or open up the pipe. If the water starts to flow, stop it immediately and give another spray or two. Wait for a few more minutes, then try again. It should have frozen.

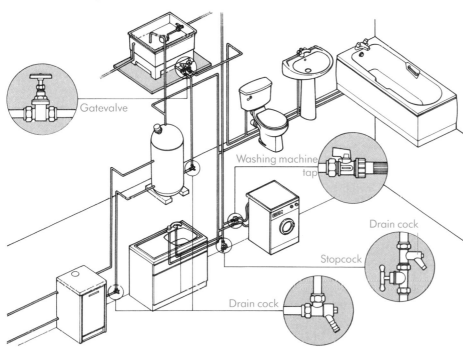

Above: Likely locations for stoptaps, gatevalves and drain cocks on a typical system.

DRIPPING TAPS

Most dripping taps can be cured simply by fitting a new washer but if this fails to cure the problem it is likely that the brass seating inside the tap has been damaged. You can buy push-in plastic seatings or re-grind the existing brass seating with a special tool. If the taps are old and worn, it may be time to think about fitting new ones.

RISING SPINDLES

The older style tap has a spindle in the middle which rises as it is turned on. After some time in service, water comes out through the top of the tap around the spindle. This is caused by wear on the packing gland. It is simple to cure once the shroud and handle have been removed.
Before carrying out any work on the taps, turn off the water.

If the tap only needs rewashering it is not essential to remove the shroud, so long as you can get a spanner underneath it to undo the head gear.

1 Put the plug in to prevent small screws being lost.
2 Remove the small grub screw from the tap head with a screwdriver and lift it off.
3 If the tap head is jammed, turn on the tap and undo the shroud. Place an open-ended spanner under the shroud and turn the tap off. The tap head should lift off as it closes down.

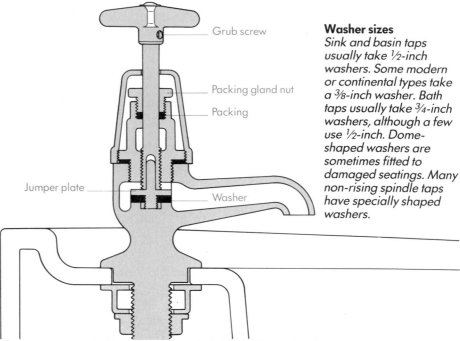

Labels: Grub screw · Packing gland nut · Packing · Jumper plate · Washer

Above: A rising spindle tap has a simple but reliable mechanism.

Washer sizes
Sink and basin taps usually take 1/2-inch washers. Some modern or continental types take a 3/8-inch washer. Bath taps usually take 3/4-inch washers, although a few use 1/2-inch. Dome-shaped washers are sometimes fitted to damaged seatings. Many non-rising spindle taps have specially shaped washers.

RESEATING
Use a reseating tool for grinding down damaged brass, to give the washer a new surface.
1 Remove the headgear of the tap and select the grinding head that best matches the washer size.
2 Screw the tool into the tap body.
3 Turn the knob or handle gently, as if turning on and off a tap. After 10 turns remove the tool and check the seating. If it is shiny, with no pits or marks, the job is done. If not, repeat.

Above: A reseating tool can give a new lease of life to an old tap.

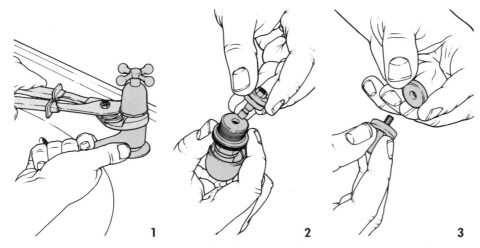

*To fit a new washer: **1** Loosen the head and remove it (there is no need to dismantle the shroud). **2** Remove the washer from the end of the jumper plate. **3** Push on the new one.*

SUPA TAPS

These taps can be rewashered without turning off the water. You need a special washer and combined jumper plate. As the sizes have changed take the old one along as a pattern.

To remove the washer, hold the nut at the top of the tap with an open-ended adjustable spanner and turn the tap as if you were turning it on. The spout will come away and, apart from a gush, the water will be sealed by a self-closing valve. Tap the anti-splash nozzle on a surface and the washer will come out.

NON-RISING SPINDLES

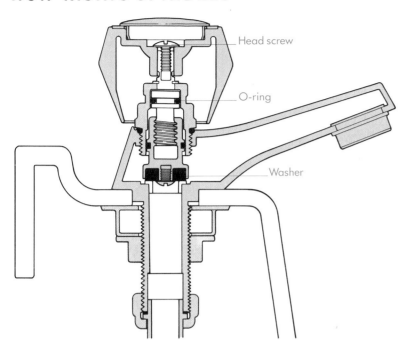

Head screw

O-ring

Washer

Above: non-rising spindle taps are neat and easy to maintain. They have shroud handles which conceal the head gear. Some are pushfit, others have a retaining screw.

There are two kinds of non-rising spindle taps. The conventional washered type; and the quarter-turn ceramic disc tap that never needs rewashering. The conventional tap is rewashered in the same way as a rising spindle tap, the only difference being the removal of the head.

Modern quarter-turn taps are fitted with ceramic discs which are claimed to be so hard they will not wear out. In theory, this means that once these taps are fitted, drips are things of the past. However, it has been known for the occasional drip, or even steady dribble, to occur. The only cure is to replace the cartridge. This is no more difficult than changing a washer.

Manufacturers will usually supply replacement parts. Be sure to ask for the correct side as they are handed right and left.

LEAKING SPINDLES

Right:
1. Freeing a tight rising spindle handle.
2. Repack the gland round the spindle.
Below:
1. Remove the disc to reveal the fixing.
2. Unscrew the headgear.
3. Slip a new O-ring on to the spindle.

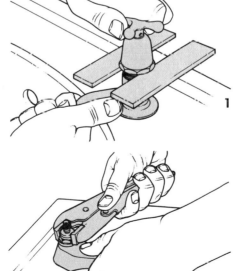

1

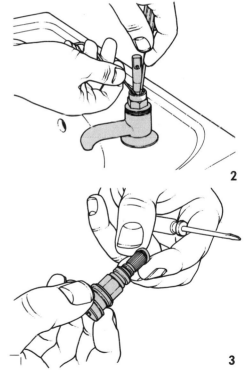

2

1

2

3

Stuffing

1 Remove the shroud. (If grips are needed, use a cloth under the jaws.)
2 Undo the gland nut at the top of the spindle and slide it off.
3 Pull some PTFE tape into a string or buy special impregnated packing material.

4 Wrap the tape around the spindle several times, pushing it down into the tap with a small screwdriver as you go.
5 Lubricate with silicone jelly before refitting the gland nut. Avoid overtightening – it will make the tap difficult to turn.

'O' rings

The spindle can be removed from the dismantled head gear by springing off the circlip and winding it out.

Flick off the rubber 'O' ring and replace it with another of the same size. Use silicone lubricant to reassemble.

BALLVALVE REPAIRS

Ballvalves are arguably the most troublesome piece of plumbing equipment ever invented. Despite some recent advancements, the perfect design is not yet with us. Few households escape the symptom of a dripping overflow for more than a few years at a time. If this tell tale warning is ignored, in the hope that it will go away, the result can be a full-bore gush of water which requires urgent action.

The first place to look for problems is a worn washer but if replacing this does not cure it look for wear, scale, grit, a leaking float and even hair line cracks in the nylon seating, probably caused by frost damage.

Most minor problems can be cured with a few tools and a little know-how but if the valve is old and worn it is usually worth replacing it with a new one. This is often a great deal easier than it first looks if the union is compatible.

Types of ballvalve

Portsmouth Made mostly of brass and used in storage tanks and WC cisterns, this type of ballvalve is found in many older homes and should be replaced during routine plumbing maintenance.

The high-pressure type is used on the mains, the low-pressure type is used on tank-fed supplies. The water flow is controlled by a piston which holds a small rubber washer against a seating. If worn or damaged by grit, the replaceable seating is often as much a cause of overflows as a worn washer.

New type (BS part two) The improved standard design now fitted on new installations to comply with current regulations has no moving parts in contact with the water and is therefore less likely to suffer from hard water scale. The overhead discharge tube also means there is a smaller risk of the outlet being submerged – a potential hazard if stored water comes into contact with mains drinking water. Rewashering is also easier and can often be carried out without tools.

Torbeck/hush-flow This plastic WC valve is now fitted on some makes of WC, mainly because it is almost silent in use. It is available as a side entry or standpipe version, depending upon where the water enters the cistern. The float arm has a tiny rubber washer on the end which blocks up a small weep hole in the front of the valve. This then forces the water to return on itself and close the valve washer by water pressure alone. Inside the valve is a fine gauze filter which prevents dirt from damaging the very delicate mechanism.

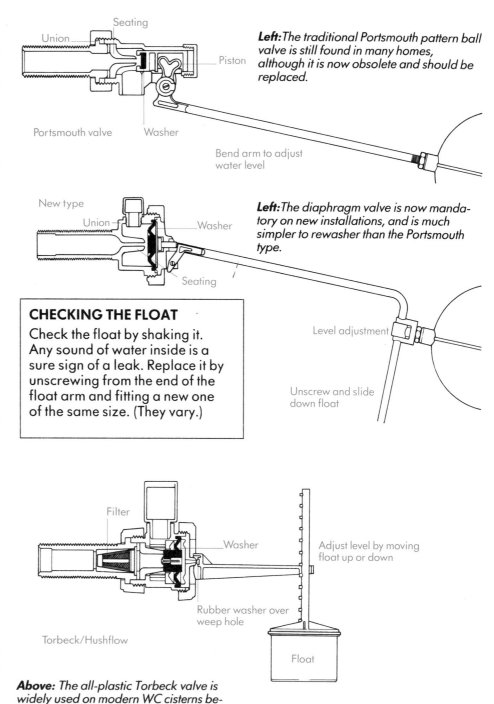

Left: The traditional Portsmouth pattern ball valve is still found in many homes, although it is now obsolete and should be replaced.

Left: The diaphragm valve is now mandatory on new installations, and is much simpler to rewasher than the Portsmouth type.

CHECKING THE FLOAT

Check the float by shaking it. Any sound of water inside is a sure sign of a leak. Replace it by unscrewing from the end of the float arm and fitting a new one of the same size. (They vary.)

Above: The all-plastic Torbeck valve is widely used on modern WC cisterns because it is almost silent in operation.

REWASHERING

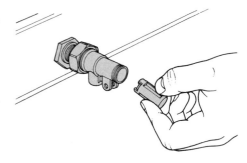

PORTSMOUTH VALVE

1 Turn off the water supply, unscrew the end cap nut and remove the split pin and float arm.

2 Take out the piston and unscrew the end section holding the washer, with a pair of grips. Push out the washer.

3 Fit a new washer and thoroughly clean off any build-up of lime scale from moving parts before reassembling them.

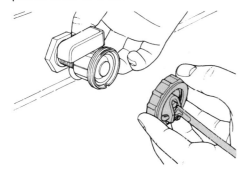

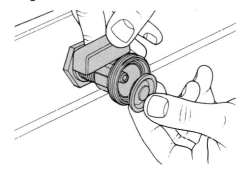

NEW TYPE DIAPHRAGM

1 Unscrew (anticlockwise) the large knurled nut on the front of the ball-valve. Remove the float and arm intact.

2 Very carefully and gently ease out the large black washer from the front of the ballvalve with a small screwdriver.

3 Fit an identical new washer in place — be careful to put the same face inwards as the one you removed.

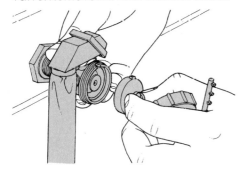

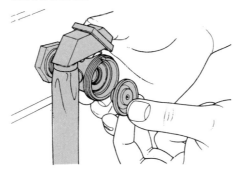

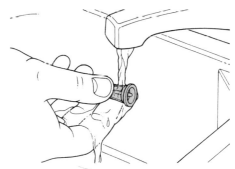

TORBECK

1 Unscrew (anticlockwise) the large nut on the front of the valve and gently pull away the whole front assembly complete with float arm.

2 Next remove the large black washer from the valve, taking careful note of how it fits over the steel pin. (There is a front and back to the washer.)

3 Clean out the fine gauze filter inside the body of the valve before reassembling the front section with a new Torbeck washer. Only a genuine Torbeck washer should be used. Adjust the water level if necessary by moving the position of the float on the arm.

The valve will not work properly if there is air in the supply pipe. If it splutters hold the float down to discharge all air before flushing the cistern and letting it fill up on its own.

REMOVING THE BALLVALVE

Working on a ballvalve is a lot easier if you remove the whole assembly first by undoing the union nut. It can then be examined for other defects such as blockages, scale and a damaged seating. If the fibre sealing washer has perished, fit a new one before replacing the valve. If the valve is badly worn, fit a new one on the old union.

BURST PIPES

Left: *A two-part Epoxy pipe and tank repair kit is a versatile measure that can be moulded around awkward joints. This is only a temporary solution, so do not be tempted to leave it.*

1: *Earthing strap*
2: *Pipe repair kit for linking cut copper pipe on each side of a length of plastic pipe*
3: *Rubber inserts for repair clamps*
4: *Epoxy putty*
5: *Plastic tape*
6: *Slip couplings*
7: *Pipe*

1 Stop the water flow by hammering the pipe flat on either side of the burst.

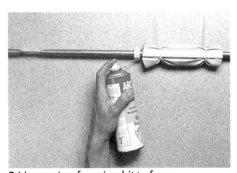

2 Use a pipe freezing kit to form an ice-plug upstream of the burst.

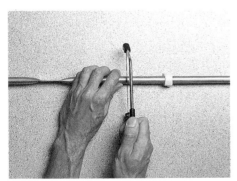

3 Cut through the pipe next to the ice-plugged section with a hacksaw.

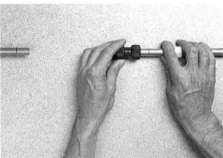

4 Fit hand-tightenable connectors to the cut ends of the pipe.

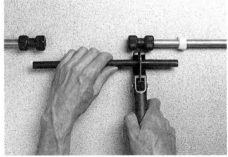

5 Measure up the length of replacement pipe needed, and cut it to length.

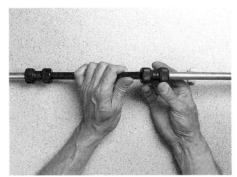

6 Slip the replacement pipe into place and tighten up the connectors.

Hammering flat

If the stopcock does not stem the flow, try running the taps to relieve the pressure on the pipe. You may then be able to wrap it with a repair bandage or old inner tube, but if neither of these are to hand hammer the pipe flat on either side of the burst. This can only be done on copper or lead, but as these are the most likely to burst it is an effective trick in most cases.

With the pipe hammered flat and the water stopped, it is possible to use an aerosol freezing kit upstream of the burst to ice-plug the pipe so it can be cut near the flattened section and repaired with a new piece.

Replacing a section

To make a permanent repair to a burst copper pipe, the damaged section must be cut back to a sound length and replaced. Copper pipe that has been frozen is likely to be enlarged along a considerable length, and you may find it has to be cut back more than you envisaged. The only way to tell is to keep cutting and trying until you reach a section that will accept the new joints.

Repair kits These come in all shapes and sizes to tackle a variety of pipes and situations. No single repair kit will cope with all types of burst, so it helps to be able to improvise.

SAFETY
Be aware of the danger from electricity. The only safe way is to turn off at the fusebox.

LEAKING RADIATORS

Close the valves on a leaky radiator.

Plug tanks with nut, bolt and washers.

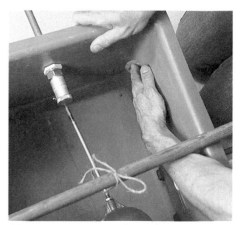

Use repair putty in awkward corners.

Sudden leaks sometimes occur in radiators as a result of corrosion. The only safe long-term solution is to replace them with new ones (see page 74) but in the meantime it is possible to carry on using the heating system if you can isolate the leaking radiator. To do this, turn off the handwheel valve on one side of the radiator. On the other side of the radiator you should find the lockshield valve, which is basically the same as the one you have already turned off except for the head. If a screw is fitted in the head, undo that first then pull the head up and off.

Turn the valve spindle with a pair of pliers or by substituting the other head. Pencil on the skirting board the number of turns it takes to close so it can be reopened by the same amount later.

Leaking tank

A leaking galvanized tank should be replaced as soon as possible with a new lightweight polythene tank, but as this is a fairly large project a temporary repair might be needed until you can manage the whole job:

1 Plug a hole by drilling (with the water drained out) through and inserting a bolt with rubber and metal washers on either side.
2 Use two-part Epoxy resin putty-type sealants on awkward corners.
3 Bend the ballvalve arm down to reduce the volume of water if the leak is nearer the top of the tank than the bottom.

Above: Lower the water level in the cistern by bending the float arm down.

SOURCING THE LEAK

Check carefully where the leak is coming from – water can be deceptive, sometimes working its way along or between surfaces to appear at a completely different point to the leak. What appears at first glance to be a leaking tank might turn out to be nothing more than a leaking joint. Tank connectors can be sealed with new washers if it is possible to take them apart, otherwise apply silicone external leak sealant around the flange.

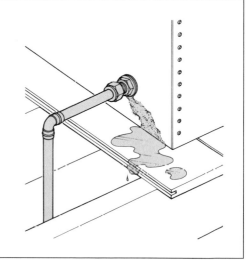

BLOCKAGES

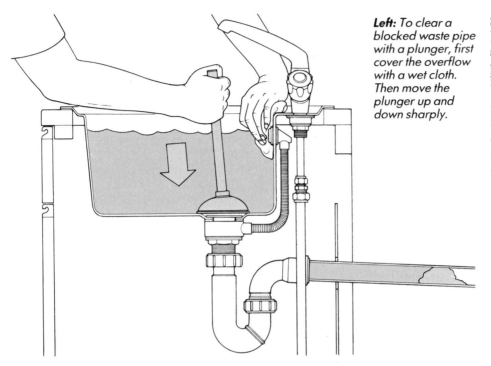

Left: *To clear a blocked waste pipe with a plunger, first cover the overflow with a wet cloth. Then move the plunger up and down sharply.*

Snake (See illustration below) For long, inaccessible wastepipes a snake is sometimes more successful, particularly on basin wastes where hair may be snagging on a pipe joint.

Feed the snake down the waste hole, turning it all the time so it travels easily around the bends. Retrieve the snake by pulling gently. If it snags, unwind it slightly rather than pulling too hard.

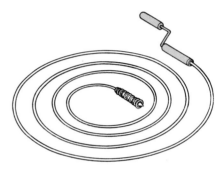

Using a sink plunger

The illustration shows a plunger being used to unblock a kitchen sink but plungers are equally useful on basins, baths and wcs.

The volume of water filling a blocked fitment and waste-pipe actually works in your favour when using a plunger, so do not bail it out. It might even help to fill it up a little, particularly with a bath. Water is not compressible, so any force placed upon one end of a full pipe by plunging must be transferred to the other end to work on the blockage, provided it has no escape route. The most common mistake is to leave the overflow pipe empty and the grille uncovered. The considerable push/pull forces built up by plunging will be wasted if they have an easy escape route up the overflow or along an air-filled pipe.

Hold a rag firmly over the overflow, or, if it is a double sink, the other waste hole as well (a three-handed job!). Then place the plunger over the waste (plug) hole and work it up and down vigorously. If you prefer, a special blockbuster gun can be used instead of a plunger, but keep the overflow and any other exits firmly covered.

BLOCKAGE CAUSED BY FAT
If the blockage is caused by congealed fat, try gently warming the trap and waste-pipe with a hair drier.

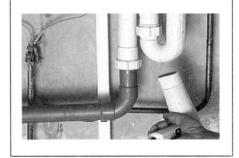

Screw rods firmly together and push down the manhole, upstream of the blockage. Often a vigorous push pull with a plunging end will clear a blockage long before the rods reach it.

If you suspect tree roots there are special revolving cutters that will remove them but contact your insurance company about a longer-term solution. Hose down the drain and surrounding area and wash the rods.

Right: *Flexible drain rods clear most blockages without fuss or mess.*

Above: *A blocked drain gully can be cleared with a blockbuster. Fit a polythene shroud before using it.*

DEALING WITH WC BLOCKAGES

Preparation

Dealing with blocked wcs cannot be anyone's idea of fun, but some blockages take only seconds to clear.

Before you suspect the loo itself of being blocked, check the outside drains are clear. Lift the manhole cover nearest the wc; if this is clear, the blockage must be between the manhole and the wc.

Before starting it is a good idea to remove any carpet around a blocked loo in case of splashes. If this is not possible, put down some old cloths or towels that you can throw away.

Below: Plunge the wc to exert a push pull which will clear all but the most stubborn blockages.

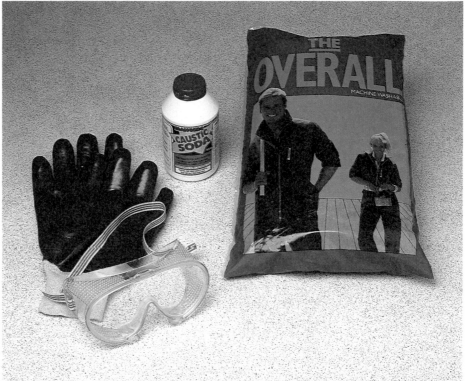

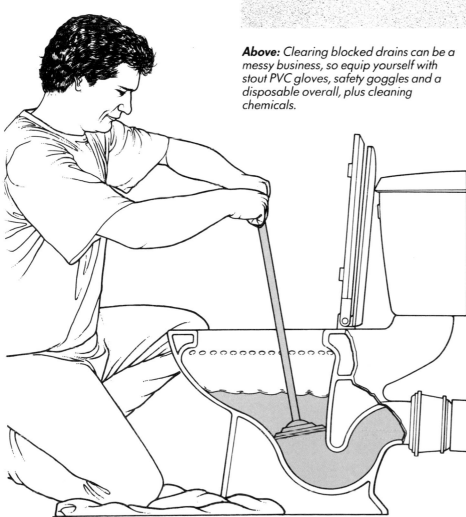

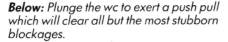

Above: Clearing blocked drains can be a messy business, so equip yourself with stout PVC gloves, safety goggles and a disposable overall, plus cleaning chemicals.

You will need an old mop or a cooper's plunger. An emergency plunger can be made from a large plastic soft drinks bottle cut in half, with a broom stick nailed in the neck of the bottle.

How to do it

Use a plunger or old mop to force the blockage around the bend. Follow this with several buckets of warm water poured in from a height. Or hire a snake wire which can be fed around the bend and down the drain.

Strong caustic soda or similar drain-clearing chemicals can sometimes be successful at clearing minor blockages, particularly if they are only making the wc slow to clear, but follow instructions carefully.

Caution

Wear gloves and goggles when handling these chemicals, and never mix them with other cleaning agents, or with each other. Open a window and leave the room while they are active. Do not use hot water with chemicals unless the instructions say you can.

AIRLOCKS

How and why they occur

Air, being lighter than water, has a natural tendency to rise in pipework. If it has no means of escape it will stay in the highest part of the system and cause an airlock.

Mains plumbing

There is sufficient pressure to force air back down the pipes and out through taps. You will see this if you drain the rising main and then turn it back on again – there will be a lot of gushing and spluttering at the taps.

Tank-fed systems

The pressure of the air is not usually enough to clear it. Sometimes you can be lucky and a small dribble of water passes the airlock and begins breaking it down, but more often than not the air will remain lodged in the pipe with the water on either side.

In a well-designed plumbing system all pipes are laid so that air will be able to escape through taps or the feed and vent pipes. Where the layout of the building makes high-spots unavoidable, small air-cocks are fitted.

Purging air

The quickest and easiest way of clearing airlocks is to blow them through with mains-pressure water by connecting a hosepipe to a mains cold water tap and the tap affected by the airlock, as illustrated. (**See the by-law note before doing this.**)

Turn on the airlocked tap first, then the mains tap. Depending on where the airlock is, the water will have to be directed along that particular pipe run. You will need a helper to hold the hosepipe while you go around turning on and off bathroom taps to try and release the air. If the airlock is on the hot pipe, it might also help to block the cylinder vent with your thumb for a minute or so but do not attach any plumbing fittings to this pipe as it is an essential safety release. Valves from the cold water tank can also be turned on and off. The success of this

depends upon the position of the airlock, but there is no harm in trying as any excess pressure will only blow the hosepipe off the taps and, at worst, splash your helper.

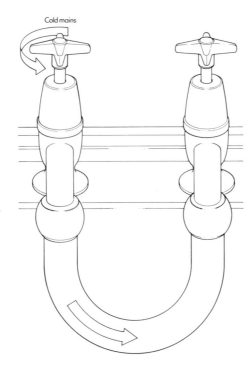

Cold mains

Central heating pipes

Often, airlocks occur when a radiator is taken off for decorating. When it is reconnected and filled it ceases to work. There are several tricks worth trying in order to clear this type of airlock:

- Turn off all radiators except the one which is airlocked. Turn on the heating system and adjust the pump speed to maximum. Leave it running for a few minutes to see if it heats up.
- Loosen a radiator valve union nut and drain off a gallon or so of water, keeping the other valve closed. Repeat the procedure with the other valve open and this one closed.
- Try back-filling the system with a mains-pressure hosepipe on one of the open valves. (**See the note on by-laws first.**)

Air in central heating systems is a common problem which, again, is likely to be a fault in the design

layout of the pipework.

If radiators develop cold areas at the top and need venting regularly, this is a sign that gas, caused by corrosion or air, is in the system. The cause of the problem is either a joint which sucks in air when the pump is switched on, or air entering through the feed or vent pipe. It might be possible to cure the problem by turning the pump speed down, or it may need some alteration in the pipework. The practical aspect of the alterations is not difficult; it usually means fitting an air separator and re-running some pipes, but the design theory can be complicated so it is best to seek professional help.

AIR AND NOISE

Release valve An automatic air-release valve can be fitted to a high spot in the pipework to release trapped air. When the air is released the valve closes under water pressure. The valve must be fitted in an upright position.

Noise Sometimes airlocks cause loud banging in the pipes as the water tries to flow. Usually this is more alarming than harmful but should be rectified by relaying the pipes.

WATER BY-LAWS

Any pipe, even a temporary one, connected between the mains and a stored water supply must be protected from the possibility of backflow. Approved hosepipe connectors with built-in backflow protection and air inlet valves might satisfy your local water by-laws but as they vary from area to area it is best to check.

The law also requires all hosepipes to be protected by such devices, either on the hose or in the supply pipe, in order to guard against contamination of mains water. The local water by-laws will give details of the type of fitting that can be used.

PUMP TROUBLES

Central heating pumps are designed to work hard and it is long bouts of inactivity that can do the damage. A jammed pump is most likely to occur on a gravity hot water heating system where the pump lies idle. On a fully-pumped system the pump works all the year round, but the motorized valve stays in one summer position and can be affected.

Some pumps have a manual restart facility to overcome sticking. As a precaution against damaging the motor, it is best to use this when starting up the system after a lay-off. If the system has been running with the pump jammed, it could already have harmed the pump but it is still worth trying to revive it.

1 With the system turned off, unscrew the cap in the middle of the pump body. Do not worry about the dribble of water that comes out.

2 Place a flat-blade screwdriver in the slot and turn it several times to free the mechanism.

3 If it feels free, start the system and it should spin. The cap can then be replaced.

4 A binding mechanism could be a sign that something inside the pump is jamming and needs flushing out.

Motorized valves

Many motorized valves have a detachable motor housing, known as the actuator. Some pull off, others have screws holding them on.

- If there is a manual lever on the valve, move it to and fro. Binding suggests some debris inside the valve body (see heating controls, page 14).
- If the valve works well, check the operation of the actuator by turning on the system and putting the programmer through its options with the boiler control off. Give the valve up to two minutes in between commands (some work slowly). If the slot can be seen turning, it is working.
- Refit the valve by lining up the spindle with the slot, and try running the system again.

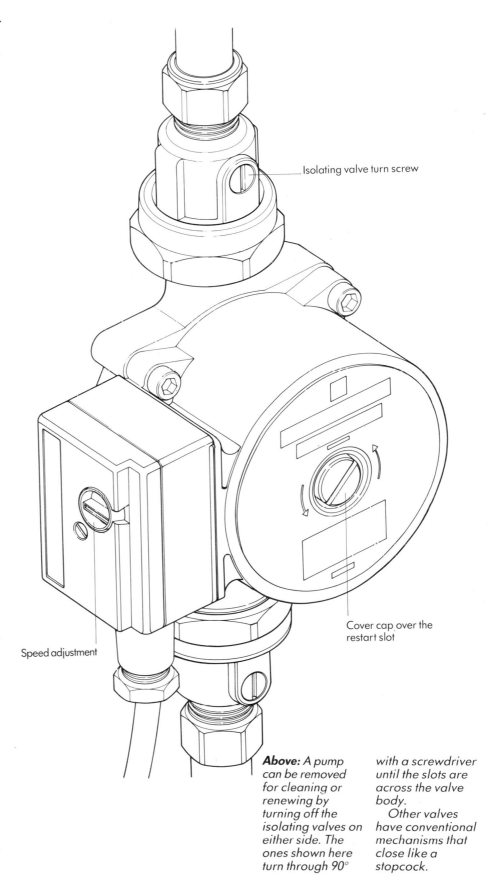

Isolating valve turn screw

Cover cap over the restart slot

Speed adjustment

Above: A pump can be removed for cleaning or renewing by turning off the isolating valves on either side. The ones shown here turn through 90° with a screwdriver until the slots are across the valve body.

Other valves have conventional mechanisms that close like a stopcock.

FITTINGS

On nearly all plumbing projects there is a choice between three different types of joints or fittings. Familiarize yourself with what is available, so that you will be able to work out which is best for you and the job you are doing. Plan ahead and write a list of the fittings you will need. Try to keep pipe runs straight and simple – there is a tendency for the inexperienced to over-complicate pipe runs.

Pipes also come in different types but here the choice for new installations is really between plastic and copper. Lead and steel are mentioned in this chapter, because it is possible that you will come across them and want to know if, and how, they can be cut and joined to. The problem of whether to use metric or imperial measurements plagues many people. The descriptions given here are how the item is sold.

Capillary fittings.
1: 15 and 22mm straight couplings. 2: 15 and 22mm 90° elbows. 3: 15 and 22mm equal tee fittings. 4: 22 × 22 × 15mm reducing tee, branch reduced. 5: 22 × 15 × 22mm reducing tee, one end reduced. 6: 22 × 15 × 15mm reducing tee, one end and branch reduced. 7: 22 × 15mm reducing coupler. 8: 15 and 22mm end caps. 9: 15mm straight tap connector. 10: 15mm bent tap connector. 11: pipe clips. 12: 15 and 22mm copper pipe and pipe clips.

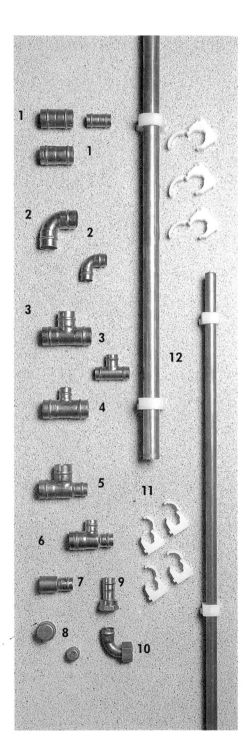

Compression fittings
1: 15mm stop end. 2: olives. 3: 15mm bent swivel tap connector. 4: 15mm straight swivel tap connector. 5: 15mm flanged tank connector. 6: 15mm × ½in straight coupler, copper × male iron. 7: 22 × 15 × 15mm reducing tee. 8: 15mm equal tee. 9: 15mm 90° elbow coupler. 10: 15mm straight coupler. 11: 15 and 22mm corrugated copper pipe. 12: 22mm × ¾in bent coupler, copper × male iron. 13: 22mm × ¾in bent coupler, copper × female iron. 14: 22mm × ¾in straight coupler, copper × male iron. 15: 22mm flanged tank connector. 16: 22 × 22 × 15mm reducing tee. 17: 22 × 15 × 22mm reducing tee. 18: 22mm equal tee. 19: 22mm 90° elbow. 20: 22mm straight coupler.

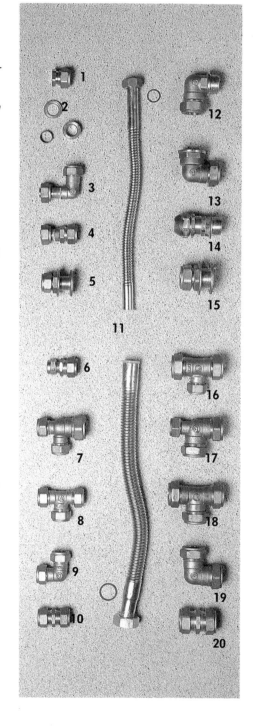

Plastic fittings
1: 22mm straight coupler. **2:** 22mm 90° elbow coupler. **3:** 22mm equal tee. **4:** 22 × 22 × 15mm reducing tee. **5:** 22mm flanged tank connector. **6:** 22mm × ¾in straight tap connector. **7:** 22mm and 15mm poly-butylene pipe. **8:** 22mm and 15mm stainless steel inserts. **9:** 22mm grab rings. **10:** 22mm end caps. **11:** 22mm sealing rings and washers. **12:** pipe clips. **13:** 15mm straight coupler. **14:** 15mm 90° elbow coupler. **15:** 15mm equal tee. **16:** sealing rings. **17:** 15mm end caps. **18:** 15mm washers. **19:** 15mm grab rings. **20:** 15mm flanged tank connector. **21:** 15mm straight tap connector. **22:** 15mm bent tap connector. **23:** 22mm stoptap. **24:** 15mm stoptap.

Valves
1: 22mm Ballofix stoptap. **2:** 15mm × ½in elbow, copper × male iron with drain cock. **3:** 15mm drain cock. **4:** Nonreturn valve. **5:** 15mm Ballofix stoptap. **6:** long tail drain cock. **7:** screw-in drain cock. **8:** 15mm stoptap. **9:** service valve **10:** 15mm washing machine stop taps. **11** and **12:** 15 and 22mm gate valves.

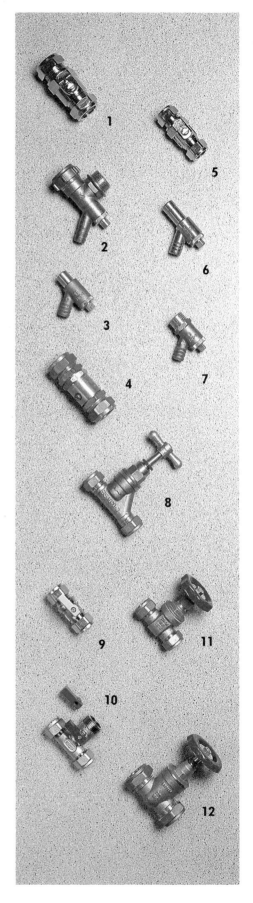

SUPPLY PIPES

Metric or imperial?

Copper went metric in 1971/2 which means imperial sizes may be found in homes built before that date. It is helpful to know this before you start, because converters will be needed for joining ¾-in to 22-mm capillary, compression or push-fit joints. For 1-in to 28-mm compression fittings you do not need converters but capillary fittings are very tight, and while it is possible to file down the pipe, it is quicker and easier to buy converters. Iron pipe is sold in imperial sizes and plastic pipe in metric.

Copper There are three grades of copper pipe available, from non-bendable to very bendable. The standard general purpose middle grade is 'Table X', which is good enough quality to give a 25-year guarantee. Copper is still the best material for hot water pipes since it has no practical upper temperature limit, but at the freezing end of the scale it is more liable to burst than plastic and should therefore be kept away from frost.

Cutting is easy with a junior hacksaw, but copper pipe cutters give a cleaner, straighter cut. Twist the cutters around the pipe, turning the knob a little at a time to close them. There is no need to break the pipe away – it will fall off when it is cut through.

Steel Mild steel pipe is no longer popular in domestic locations, because it is difficult to work and not very neat. Where it is already installed it can be altered at joins using male or female fittings of brass or plastic and plastic or stainless steel pipe. Copper pipe should not be joined to galvanized iron as it sets up a corrosive action known as electrolysis. Mild steel pipe can be cut with a full-size hacksaw or, with patience, even a junior hacksaw.

If you are simply removing steel pipe, an electric angle grinder with a wheel for cutting steel is the fastest method, but wear eye protection as this process can be dangerous.

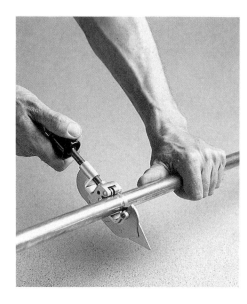

Above: Cut copper pipe easily and accurately using pipe cutters, holding the pipe lightly but firmly.

Above: Cut polybutylene pipe to length using the special cutting pliers to ensure that the cut is square.

Plastic Polybutylene supply pipe is becoming more popular. Its chief advantages are:
- Flexibility – it can be bent and run under floorboards more easily.
- Frost damage resistance – it is unlikely to burst when frozen.
- Heat retention – it still needs insulating.
- Quieter – a feature often overlooked which can be important on mains plumbing running through bedrooms.

Plastic also has some limitations:
- Affected by sunlight – it must be covered outdoors.
- Non-conductor of electricity – which is no bad thing, but it breaks the continuity of earth bonding and therefore needs bypass linkages.
- Unsuitable for connection to boilers and water heaters – at least 1m (3 ft 3-in) of copper must be used first.
- Not presently accepted for all heating system service contracts – but this may change.

Cutting and joining plastic pipes

Polybutylene is sold in 3-metre lengths or rolls of up to 100 metres. Cut it with a junior hacksaw or a special snipper which makes a neater square cut needing no further preparation.

The ends of the pipe must be lined with stainless steel inserts to prevent distortion when joining.

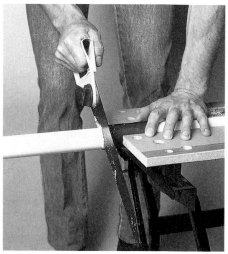

Above: Cut large-diameter plastic waste pipes with a general-purpose saw.

The Scratch Test Check which type of pipe you have in your house by scratching off a bit of paint. Lead has a very soft and shiny surface when scratched but this dulls. Steel is silvery or black and is very hard to scratch. Copper is often black or even green with age but reveals its true colour when scratched.

Above: Use a junior or full-sized hacksaw to cut through mild steel piping.

Lead pipe – Is it a health hazard?

Lead pipe is now outlawed for new supply pipes in the UK and cannot be used in repairs or joints. However, many homes still have lead pipes, recognizable by their long bulbous joints. The risk to health is a cause of concern to a growing number of people.

The official thinking is that lead is only a significant hazard in soft-water areas, where the water is acidic enough to draw lead out into the drinking supplies. Your water authority will be able to advise on local conditions and give details of any grants available for renewing the pipe with a safer alternative.

As a precaution, anyone with lead pipes to their drinking tap should run some water first thing in the morning before drinking any water. Concentrations are likely to be highest where water has been static for several hours. To avoid wasting water, the wc can be flushed and washing water can be run to get it moving along the mains pipe.

Since 1989 it has also become illegal to use lead solder in drinking supplies, which is an indication of official concern over even small amounts of lead in the plumbing system. Compression fittings or special lead-free solder fittings are safe alternatives. Look for the lead-free symbol (see the illustration below) before buying.

If you have to join up or repair lead pipe with another material, special compression type converters should be used; these have rubber seals and grab-rings and need only a pair of grips to tighten them.

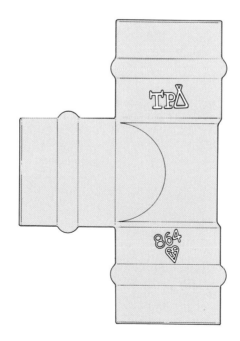

Above: Lead pipe can be recognised by its slow bends and bulbous joints. It should be replaced where possible by copper pipe.

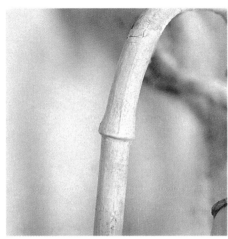

Above: Lead-free joints are now mandatory on copper pipes. These can be plastic push-fit or compression but if you prefer to use solder joints look for the lead-free symbol. This ensures suitability for drinking water and will satisfy the water authority inspector.

Water Filters

Even removing all the lead pipes in your house will not completely solve the problem of contamination as the underground supply pipe might still be lead. There are also a number of other contaminants that can be found in drinking water and these are causing as much concern. Organisations such as Friends of the Earth have up-to-date information about the concentration of contaminants throughout the country.

One way to guard against contaminants is to use a water filter. There are several types but it is advisable to check that they will filter out the particular contaminants you are concerned about.

Jug-type filters Although jug filters have been around since Victorian times the modern industrial environment has thrown up such a variety of chemicals it is asking a lot of any filter to remove them all. Nevertheless, jug filters are surprisingly effective for a short while. The secret is the fact that they allow only small quantities of water to filter through over several hours. They can normally filter out tastes and smells through their activated carbon and suspended solids through their micro mesh. The solids include lead, and they may also take out nitrates and bacteria but the continuing ability to do this depends upon replacing the filter element regularly.

Plumbed-in filters These can be fitted on to the drinking supply pipe to the tap but are generally not as effective because water is forced through them too quickly.

A finer filter designed to strain down to one micron or less will be more effective but the quantity of water it can handle is so small that a special drinking-water-only tap will be needed. Some kits come complete with filter and tap and are designed for easy fitting, others need plumbing in with conventional fittings but both types are well within the scope of the DIY plumber.

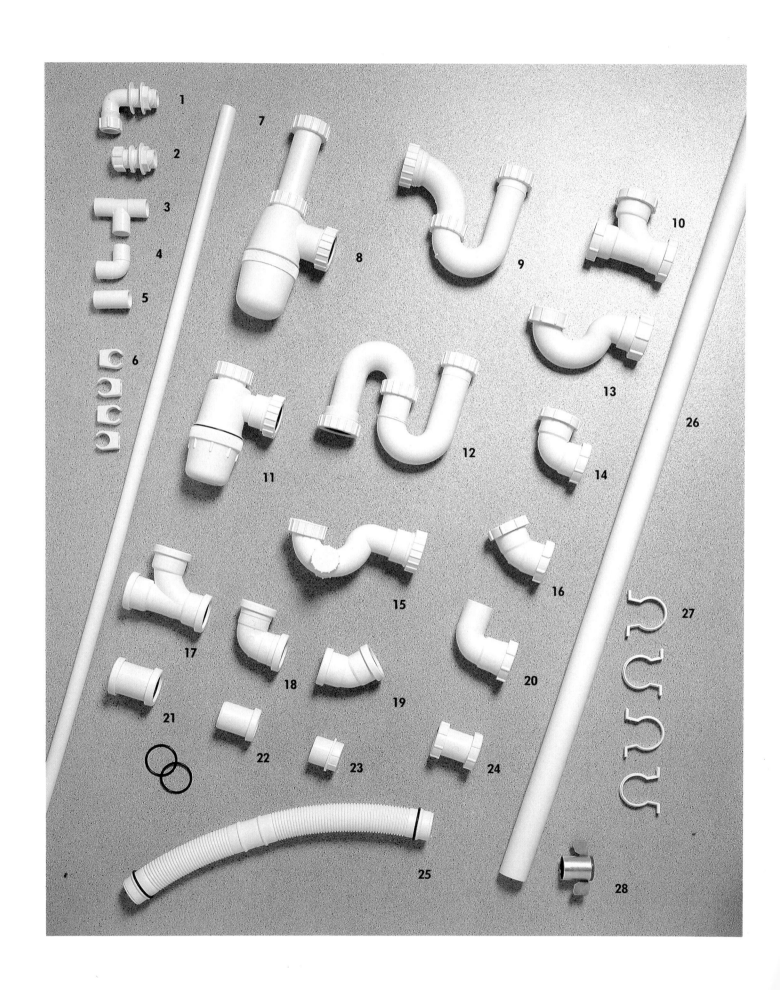

A leak on a wc outlet is not only unpleasant but also a health hazard. To ensure a good seal it is important to make sure that you choose the right fitting for the pipe.

New wcs

These have horizontal outlets which should be attached to a connector suitable for the pipe. This can either be straight out through the wall (P or horizontal trap) or down through the floor (S trap).

Horizontal outlets. On a new soil pipe this should fall at 2½° gradient down to the vertical section of the soil stack.

On an older soil pipe previously connected to a P trap pan this angle will be steeper: a 14° fitting may be needed although there are many variations. If problems arise a fitting adjustable between 0° and 25° can be used.

Where the wc pan is further out from the wall than allowed for by the fitting, an extension piece can be fitted between the pan connector and the soil branch pipe. The extension piece can be cut to length with a multipurpose saw.

Special Adaptors. The usual soil pipe is 4″ internal diameter but some were made in 3½″ or even 3″. Adaptors are made but they are not a stock item so it is worth measuring the soil pipe first and ordering the part. The outside diameter of a cast-iron pipe is usually about ½″ more than the internal bore.

90° bends

These can be used to convert a horizontal outlet to an S trap or a side outlet P trap. The side pipe should still fall at 2½° or more to the vertical section.

Overflow fittings
1: 90° tank connector. 2: straight tank connector. 3: 90° tee. 4: 90° elbow. 5: straight connector. 6: pipe clips. 7: 22mm overflow pipe.

Traps and waste fittings
8: bottle P-trap with adjustable neck. 9: tubular swivel-neck P-trap. 10 and 17: swept tee conectors. 11: bottle P-trap. 12: tubular swivel-neck S-trap. 13 and 15: shallow seal tubular traps. 14 and 18: 90° elbow couplers. 16 and 19: 135° couplers. 20: Universal 90° elbow coupler. 21 to 24: straight couplers 25: flexible waste pipe. 26: 32mm waste pipe. 27: pipe clips. 28: Tapering and deburring tool.

WC pan connectors
1: 90° bend to convert horizontal outlet of BS5503 pan to S-trap or to left or right-hand P-trap. 2: extension piece, for connecting another pan connector to the soil pipe. 3: 14° bend connector, to convert horizontal outlet of BS5503 pan to P-trap. 4: straight connector, for linking pan outlets of various types to soil pipes.

GUTTERING

Modern PVC gutter is both light-weight and durable making it the ideal replacement for rusing cast iron.

All cast-iron fittings and sections are replicated in plastic so it should be possible to copy the existing system.

Nonstandard fittings

There are a few nonstandard fittings, such as odd angle brackets to go around bay windows. Some leading manufacturers will make one-off pieces to order if you send them a detailed drawing of what is required. If you require an odd angle and are not sure how to measure it send a cardboard template.

Adhesives

External PVC gutters and down pipes are intended to be push-fit. Adhesives are not usually used but on odd occasions it might be necessary to solvent-weld a shoe onto the bottom of the pipe if no suitable bracket fixing can be made. Solvent-weld cement is used for making certain fittings to waste pipes (see page 47).

Expansion and contraction

This takes place within each fitting. Make sure that gutters and pipes are inserted only up to the line and not all the way to the stop end. Gutter support brackets are needed every 1000mm (3ft), down pipe brackets every 1.6m (5ft).

Beating the Burglar Special slippery non-drying paint for use on cast-iron rainwater and soil pipes is available to deter burglars from climbing them. Plastic pipes, being

Guttering *(left)*
1: *90° angle.* **2:** *135° angle.* **3:** *gutter section with supporting bracket and running outlet.* **4:** *stopend outlet.* **5:** *stopend.* **6:** *Gutter support bracket.* **7:** *fixed union.*

Downpipes *(right)*
1: *90° bend.* **2:** *pipe bracket.* **3:** *hopper head with downpipe section and pipe bracket.* **4:** *and* **5:** *135° offset bends.* **6:** *spigot and socket for joining pipe.* **7:** *rainwater shoe.*

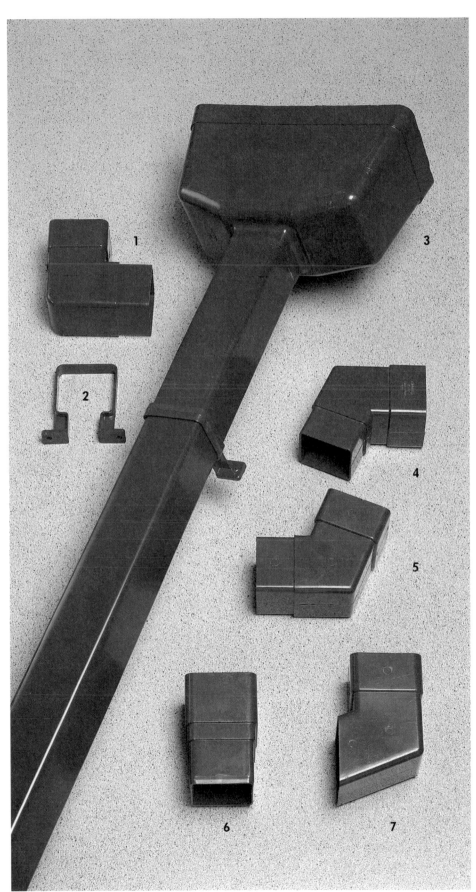

inherently less robust, are a deterrent in themselves. This is a desirable feature when it comes to home security but if you are considering using them to secure a tower scaffold or ladder, think again: they are not designed to take any strain. All ladders and towers should be secured with vine eyes or screw hooks driven directly into wall plugs or sound facia boards. See page 18.

Snow guards These are a useful feature, particularly above conservatories or lightweight lean-tos.

THE TECHNIQUES

The level of skill needed to join and bend pipes is now considerably less than it was even a few years ago. Once the basic techniques have been mastered, a whole range of projects are suddenly opened up. To begin with it is best to gain confidence on a smaller project, such as fitting an outside tap. Provided the instructions are followed, perfect leak-free joints should be achieved every time.

If a joint does leak, there must be a reason. It sounds obvious but it is surprising how many people smear sealants around fittings rather than looking to see what is wrong. Bear in mind that water can run down pipes and drip from the outside of fittings that are sound. If this is difficult to see, wrap tissue around the pipes and fittings and wait to see which show signs of moisture.

COMPRESSION JOINTS

Brass compression joints can be used on copper, plastic or stainless steel pipework up to any pressure likely to be found in domestic plumbing.

They have a proven record and are widely used by professionals. They

to an existing installation, remove traces of paint and so on with some fine emery cloth. Check that the ends of the pipe are round and remove burrs which might prevent the ring from going on. If plastic pipe is used, a metal stiffener must be pushed into each end of the pipe.

As the seal is brass against brass, smear a little Fernox XLS leak sealant or Hawk White jointing compound around the inside mouth of the fitting before assembly.

The reduced end is like a standard compression fitting and the pipe can be inserted in the usual way.

1 Thread the nuts and rings over the cut pipe ends carefully and push the pipes into the fitting. Make sure they meet the internal stops and are accurately aligned.

2 After getting the feel of compression joints it is possible to push the pipe in without dismantling, but be sure it goes right in before tightening the nuts by hand.

3 Tighten each nut in turn with a spanner until it feels firm. Do not overtighten or you may damage the thread — one turn past hand-tight is about right.

work by the nut compressing a brass or copper ring around the pipework when it is tightened. This grabs the pipe and forms a watertight seal.

If the joint needs dismantling it is a simple matter of undoing the nut, which makes it the ideal joint for valves and other components that might need removing for servicing or replacement. Another advantage of these fittings is that they can be made even when there are traces of water in the pipe – something that is impossible with solder fittings. If a leak does occur on a compression joint, do not overtighten it.

Preparation

With all joints, preparing the pipe ends is important. If you are joining

Reducing inserts

The reducing insert is a three-piece kit which replaces the existing ring in the compression fitting and makes it possible to fit a smaller pipe. The nut is also adapted by a similar arrangement and a new ring is supplied. This can save time and trouble, especially if you find a fitting unsuitable.

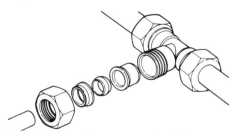

Reducing insert for compression fitting.

STOPPING DRIPS

Although extra sealant is not normally required on compression fittings, it is difficult to stop a drip any other way. One trick is to dismantle the fitting and wrap a couple of turns of PTFE tape around the face of the ring (not the threads).

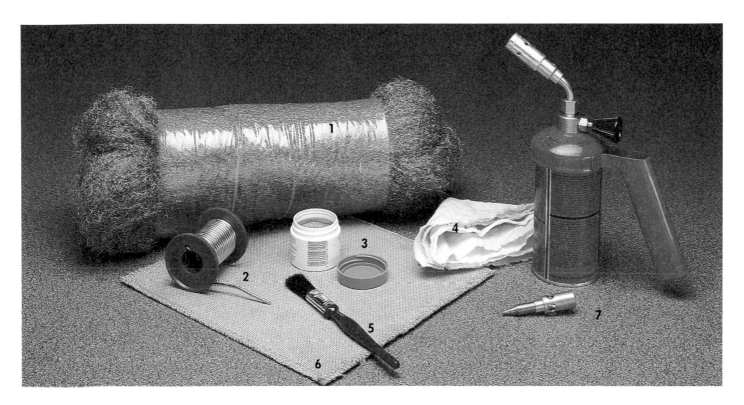

1: Steel wool 2: Solder 3: Flux 4: Cloth for wiping joints 5: Flux brush 6: Heat-resistant mat 7: Blowlamp and nozzle.

SOLDER JOINTS

Absolute cleanliness and the complete absence of water in the pipework are essential. If either of these are not possible, use another type of fitting.

Pipe ends and the insides of fittings must be shiny. Polish away any tarnishing on the pipe end and on the inside of the fitting with steel wool.

Flux

This helps the solder run evenly around the joint. Self-cleaning flux avoids the need for polishing, but it does no harm to clean anyway. Apply the flux sparingly with a small brush (not your finger), around the inside of the fitting and the outside of the pipe. Excess flux must be removed, after soldering the joint, by wiping with a damp cloth.

Assembly

Make sure when assembling the joint that the pipes go right up to the internal stops, then heat each end at a time with a blowlamp until a continuous ring of solder appears around the mouth. Withdraw the heat as soon as all the ends have been heated. Do not disturb until the joint has cooled. If the joint leaks, drain, reclean, reflux and reheat. Extra solder can be melted on the hot end.

SAFETY

Take care when working with a blowlamp. In particular, remember these points:

- Remove anything inflammable from the immediate area.
- Protect surfaces with a glassfibre mat.
- Keep a fire extinguisher and a bucket of water handy. If you burn your hand, plunge it in the water and keep it there until the pain goes.
- Avoid damage to wiring – it is easily melted. Check the area immediately after use, and again later on.
- Never leave a burning lamp unattended.
- Never store or change gas cylinders in the same room as a flame.

How capillary soldering works

The fine tolerance between the pipe and fitting draws the molten solder into all the gaps as it is heated. If the gap is too large or small the solder might not fill it effectively. It is essential to have perfectly rounded pipes and fittings.

Checklist for successful soldering of copper pipes and fittings.

1: Clean the pipes and fittings thoroughly.

2: Make sure there is no water in the pipes and that none can run down during soldering.

3: Apply flux to all surfaces to be soldered.

4: Heat the fittings at the mouths with a blowlamp or electric soldering tongs.

5: As soon as the solder appears remove the heat and leave the joint to set.

6: Do not mix lead-free solder and lead solder in the same joint, they have different melting temperatures.

7: Solder fittings can be heated for dismantling and reused but reflux them and add a little extra solder by melting it onto the mouth of the fitting when it is hot.

PUSH-FIT JOINTS

Above: Insert liners into plastic pipe ends.

Above: Push the pipe into the end of the fitting.

Main advantages:

- No skill needed.
- Only a pipe cutter required.
- Joints will rotate on the pipe without affecting the seal.
- Joints can be removed easily.
- Joins on to inaccessible pipes, where a spanner or a blowlamp cannot be used.

Main disadvantages:

- Temperature limitations.
- Breaks earth continuity.
- Can be tampered with by children.
- Bulky and obtrusive fittings.
- Can slip off chrome-plated or stainless steel tube if water hammer is present in the system.

Which pipe?

Although copper and stainless steel can be used, the ideal pipe for plastic push-fittings is plastic, which gives the grab-rings a softer surface to 'grab'. Grab-rings can be removed with pliers but should not then be reused. Using plastic pipe avoids the risk of damaging the fittings, but remember that there are positions where plastic pipe should not be used, such as for vent pipes and for direct connections to boilers.

Liners

Always fit liners into plastic pipe ends. Check that all metal pipe ends are well rounded and free from burrs which can damage the 'O' ring. The best way to cut pipes is with a pipe cutter rather than a junior hacksaw: it gives a squarer cut and leaves cleaner, less jagged edges. If the pipe needs to be removed, unscrew the nut before pulling it out. Keep the joints clean by storing them in a polythene bag.

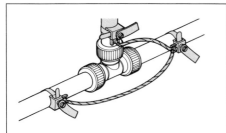

SAFETY
Where a plastic joint or pipe is fitted in between lengths of metal pipe, an earthing strap must be fitted to each pipe, linked by 6mm² earth wire.

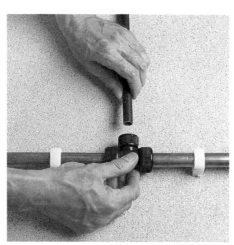

Above: Plastic push-fittings can be used to connect copper pipes to each other and to polybutylene. A steel liner is used only in the polybutylene pipe.

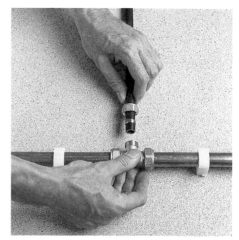

Above: Alternatively, you can use the standard brass compression fittings. Slide the cap nut and olive on to the polybutylene pipe before inserting the steel liner.

THREADED JOINTS

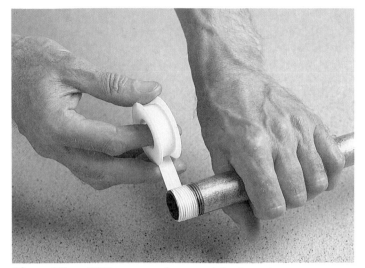

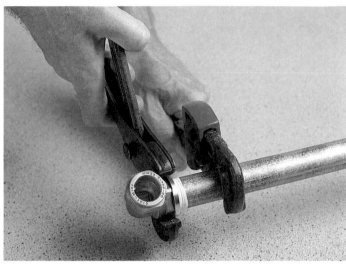

Above: Wrap PTFE tape evenly around the threads.

Above: Hold the pipe and screw on the threaded fitting.

Threaded connections are common on such items as cast-iron boilers, as well as steel panel radiators and copper cylinders. They are also found on taps and ballvalves. These threads are parallel, which means they remain at the same diameter along their entire length. Threads are also found on old pipework and fittings as tapered threads, which tighten as you screw them up. If they are overtightened they can split the iron fittings open.

Joining or teeing off

Avoid the need to cut new threads by joining to existing threaded ends and fittings with compression joints. These joints are confusingly described as either male or female 'iron' BSP (British Standard Pipe size) but in fact are made from brass.

Hemp joints

Threaded pipes were sealed with hemp and linseed oil based compounds such as Boss white. Hemp is now outlawed on drinking and gas supplies. When coal gas was used pipes were sealed with Boss white and hemp and because the gas was moist it worked well. Natural gas is dry and hemp joints subsequently leak. PTFE tape is the modern substitute and requires no compounds or lubrication.

Wrap PTFE tape, clockwise, around the male threads in overlapping turns until it is between four and six layers thick.

Screw the thread and fitting together using Stillsons or a self-gripping pipe wrench.

Brass threads, such as taps, can be joined to pipes by a swivel connector with a fibre washer placed between the thread end and the fitting flange. Sometimes a nut and ring can be used to make a compression fitting.

CHROME OR BRASS

On chrome or brass, roughen the thread slightly with a junior hacksaw to prevent the PTFE tape from sliding up.

REPLACING A SECTION

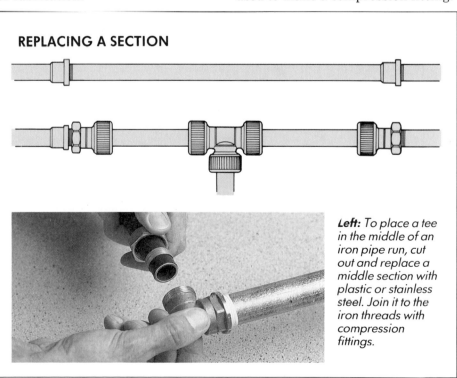

Left: To place a tee in the middle of an iron pipe run, cut out and replace a middle section with plastic or stainless steel. Join it to the iron threads with compression fittings.

WASTE-PIPE JOINING

There are three different types of joint used on plastic waste-pipe. Before joining to any existing pipe see pages 38-41 regarding types of pipe and fittings, as not all are compatible. Your new pipe and fittings should all be from the same range and, therefore, compatible.

Clean pipes All pipe should be clean and cut squarely at the ends. Pipe used in push-fit joints must be slightly tapered at the end with a file to prevent dislodging the rubber seals. Solvent-welded pipe and joints should be cleaned with a chemical sold with the system.

Expansion joints Plastic pipes expand when hot. To prevent buckling, an expansion joint must be used on lengths over 1m (3 ft) which have two fixed ends. Pipes must also be supported by clips at 500-mm (18-in) intervals to prevent sagging. On vertical runs clip every 2m (6 ft).

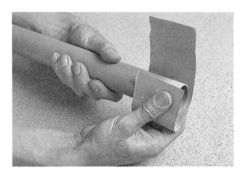

SOLVENT WELD

1 Clean mating parts with chemical cleaner or roughen with glasspaper.

2 Apply a coat of solvent weld to both surfaces.

3 Push the pipe into the socket, twisting slightly for a good seal.

PUSH FIT

1 Clean and taper the pipe end to a 45° angle using the deburring tool.

2 Smear silicone lubricant on the rubber seal before assembling.

3 Mark the pipe with a pen. Withdraw it 3mm (⅛ in) for expansion.

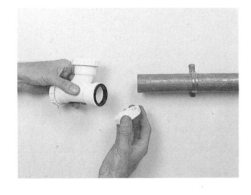

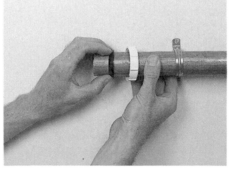

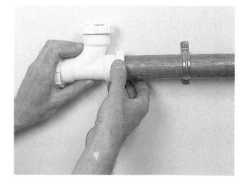

MECHANICAL

1 When purchased, the tapered ring is often jammed inside the fitting.

2 Thread on the back nut, the anti-rotation ring and the rubber seal.

3 Insert the pipe and tighten the nut by hand only; grips may distort it.

JOINING PLASTIC TO METAL

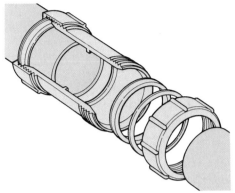

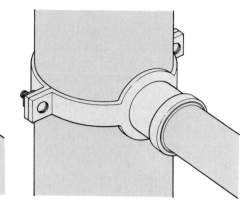

Lead This can be joined to plastic with a mechanical fitting. You will probably have to file or bell out the pipe end to fit the joint.

A push-fit joint This joint, with a special red seal, is often used on copper and provides expansion. Alternatively, use a mechanical fitting.

A special strap-on boss This has a rubber seal and can be used to join a plastic pipe into a cast-iron soil pipe. Cut the hole with a quality hole saw.

Opposite connections on soil stacks can cause cross-flow and blockages. To guard against this problem, opposite connections must not be made in the area 200mm (8 in) below a branch. Plastic soil pipe can be put into cast-iron collars using a caulking collar and plastic lead cold sealing compound.

SOIL PIPES

Plastic soil pipes These are really only larger versions of waste-pipes and can be joined by solvent weld or push-fit. Use push-fit joints on branches and bends if you want to have a second chance at alignment.

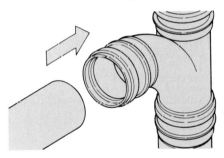

Push-fit rubber seals These should be used to join waste-pipes to ready-made bosses to allow for expansion and easy removal.

CONNECTIONS
To avoid blockages and siphoning of traps the connections to the soil pipe should be made with care and forethought.

Make all connections into the vertical pipe, never into a horizontal branch.

Observe the dimensions and rules about opposing pipes shown in the illustration.

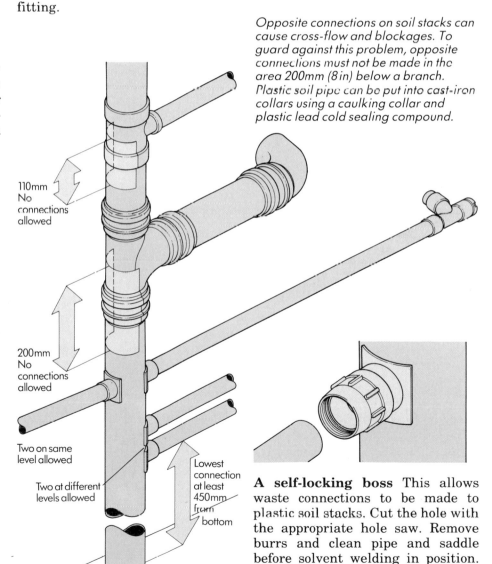

110mm No connections allowed

200mm No connections allowed

Two on same level allowed

Two at different levels allowed

Lowest connection at least 450mm from bottom

A self-locking boss This allows waste connections to be made to plastic soil stacks. Cut the hole with the appropriate hole saw. Remove burrs and clean pipe and saddle before solvent welding in position. Ensure that the curve of the saddle 'aligns' with that of the pipe.

RUNNING PIPES

Supporting

Support pipes to prevent them sagging when full of water and placing a strain on the joints, but never use pipes to support anything else (such as a basin).

Supply pipes are also likely to knock when water is turned off at the taps if adequate pipe clips are not used. Often-neglected places for clips are under floorboards, where pipes have been threaded through in line with joists, and in lofts, where pipes are laid over joists.

Passing through

Protect pipes passing through walls or wooden joists with sleeving to prevent noises and to guard against possible damage caused by rubbing during expansion.

Never bury a pipe in sand and cement without wrapping it in insulation or corrosion-resistant tape first.

All pipes, especially gas, must be sleeved with larger pipe where they pass through cavity walls, so that any leaks are discharged outside the cavity and can be detected immediately.

Lifting boards

Being careful of cables and pipes, cut floorboards centrally over joists using a circular power saw set to the depth of the board. Avoid hitting nails, which will ruin the blade. Alternatively, use a hand saw – preferably a special floorboard type with teeth around its nose.

Tongued and grooved boards need cutting down each side to release them from adjoining boards. A hammer and electrician's bolster can be used to gently split through them.

CUTTING A LINE IN A JOIST

If you do not have a suitable saw, use a fine drill to drill a series of close holes all along a line over a joist. Mark the drill with tape so it does not go any deeper than the board.

Above: *Pipes running parallel with joists can be supported on special timber inserts or clipped to the side. Leave space for insulation if needed.*

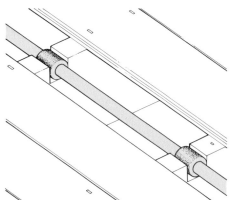

Above: *Sleeve pipes through joists with insulation material to prevent noises.*

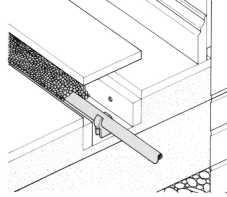

Above: *A pipe laid through a cement floor should be ducted or well insulated.*

Above: *Use a claw hammer and electrician's bolster to lever up floorboards gently. For safety's sake remove nails immediately.*

BENDING PIPES

Spring-bending

A bending spring is designed to prevent the walls of the pipe collapsing, so the correct size for the pipe is essential.

1 Lightly oil a new spring and tie a long piece of string to the end of it so that it can be retrieved after the bend is made.

2 Position the spring inside the bend so the pipe is well supported around its entire circumference. The string can be marked so you know where the spring is in relation to the pipe.

3 To release tension on the spring and make withdrawal easier, slightly overbend the pipe and then bend it back to the desired position.

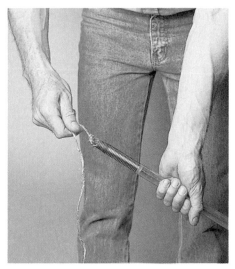

If a pipe cutter was used, deburr the end before inserting the spring.

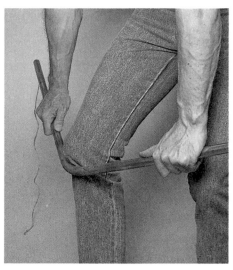

Pull a spring bend gently around the knee until it is slightly over bent. Then bend back.

Line up the mark with the centre of the former channel using an offcut of pipe.

Push the bender arm gently around until the desired angle has been formed.

Machine pipe-bending

Pipe-bending machines give a more uniform and tighter bend than springs, and are well worth hiring for the larger project. They take a little practice to begin with but once mastered are quick and easy to use. Start with a simple bend and progress to double-bend offsets.

One quirk of the machine method is that it holds one end of the pipe stationary while pulling the free end around the former, unlike the spring which pulls both ends evenly. This puts all the distance saved from going around the bend at the front end of the pipe. For anyone not intent upon a career in plumbing it is not worth calculating the gain in order to save a couple of inches of copper pipe. Far better to trim it after the bend has been made.

1 Mark out the distance from the last fitting to the centre of the pipe on the bent run.

2 Place the pipe in the former and flip over the hook to retain the pipe.

3 Line up the mark on the pipe so it is exactly in line with the centre of the 90° angle. An off-cut of pipe can be used to do this.

4 Place the backslide under the wheel and pull the bending arm around the former until the desired angle is reached.

ANNEALING

It is hard to bend 22-mm and 28-mm pipes with a spring. To make them easier, the copper pipe can be annealed first.

Heat the area where the bend is to be made over a gas ring or by using a blowlamp. Let the pipe glow cherry-red, then allow it to cool thoroughly before inserting the spring and bending.

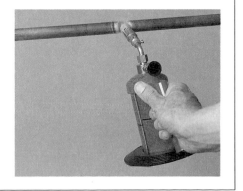

BATHROOM PROJECTS

Fitting your own bathroom suite might seem like being thrown in at the deep end, but even though it appears to be an ambitious project it is a lot more straightforward than many people might imagine. Each bathroom fitment, no matter how big or small, requires only three connections to link it to the plumbing. Taking each fitment on its own, you will find there is nothing particularly daunting about any of them.

The problems begin when they are all tackled together. With the bathroom out of action for days on end, and patience wearing thin, the pressure is on to get the job finished – and that is where quality tails off. Much of this can be avoided by planning and preparation. Leave the disconnection of the old fitments until the last possible moment and aim to bring each new fitment 'on stream' before starting the next.

Preparation

The new fitments should be fully assembled, including taps and wastes, before any work in the bathroom begins. This includes fitting flexi connectors to the taps, and traps to the wastes.

Make a careful sketch and measurement of the intended pipe runs and write a list of fittings and accessories.

Purchase sets of valves so that each fitment can be turned off individually, to allow problems to be dealt with without turning everything off.

Measuring up

Make a sketch of your bathroom to scale, and juggle around with paper shapes until you come up with a workable scheme. Then consider how to run the pipes. If you find that your layout poses some awkward problems, such as running waste-pipes uphill, it will be back to the drawing board. Good ideas are often slow to mature; so do not rush them. The working areas around fitments are suggested for comfort, and can overlap – provided two people are not sharing the bathroom at the same time.

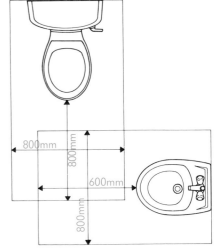

Left: *renovating a bathroom with an elegant, new, modern suite such as this is not so daunting a project for the DIY plumber as it might at first seem.*

Below: *Comfortable space around each fitment is given in mm. The spaces can overlap.*

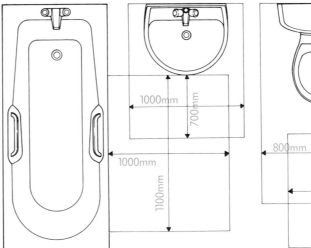

1000mm
700mm
1000mm
1100mm
800mm
800mm
600mm
800mm

The law

Apart from the drainage mentioned on page 16, the building by-laws also require bathrooms and WCs to be ventilated. A WC must not open directly on to a kitchen or eating area for obvious reasons of hygiene but must be separated by a ventilated lobby. Details are available from your local authority building control office.

Regulations

The water by-laws The installation of pipes and fittings is governed by these regulations – a copy is available from your local water authority.

Electrical safety regulations Also of great importance in bathrooms are the IEE (Institute of Electrical Engineers) regulations – your local library or council should have a copy

of the 15th edition. The main rules are: No socket outlets (except for shaver supply units) are allowed; switches within 2.5m (8ft) of a bath or shower must be of the pull-cord type; all metal plumbing including iron and steel baths and central heating radiators must be earth-bonded. No socket outlet (except as above) may be within 2.5m of a shower fitted in a bedroom.

WATER SUPPLIES AND WASTES

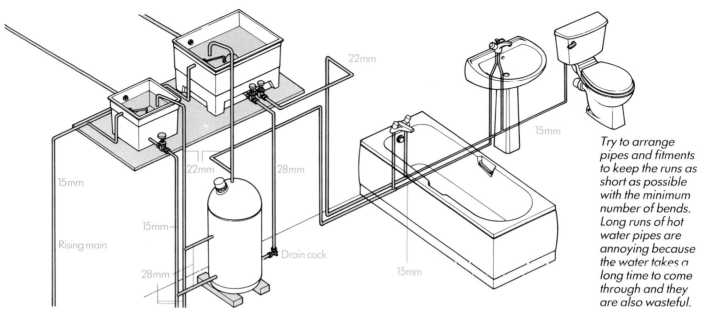

22mm

15mm

22mm

28mm

15mm

Rising main

28mm

Drain cock

15mm

Try to arrange pipes and fitments to keep the runs as short as possible with the minimum number of bends. Long runs of hot water pipes are annoying because the water takes a long time to come through and they are also wasteful.

Supplies

With the exception of an ascending spray bidet or manual shower, all fitments on a tank fed system can be supplied from the same pair of 22-mm hot and cold pipes.

After serving the bath, the pipes can be reduced to 15-mm for all the other fitments.

Thermostatic showers These must have hot coming in on the left and cold on the right, but wherever practicable all tap connections should also follow this convention.

If this is difficult to achieve with the pipe runs, a last-minute swap-over can be made with flexi tap connectors.

Mains cold water If your bathroom taps are not the type where the hot and cold water is mixed before it leaves the tap, this can be used to supply bathroom taps directly.

Mains water should not be used to supply a shower unless both hot and cold are mains-fed and the shower mixer is suitable for high pressure.

Waste

Although the joints are simple to make, running waste-pipes is often more difficult than running the supplies. The need to maintain a continuous gentle fall, and the larger diameter of the pipes, means they cannot be run through notches across floor joists. If they run below floorboards it can only be in the same direction as the joists, or boxed-in below the ceiling.

Easy flow Pipe runs must be designed to offer as little resistance to the waste water as possible, and also to prevent blockages forming. Where branches are used to join one flow into another, make sure the sweep is in the direction of the flow. Look for flow arrows stamped on the side of some fittings.

WC waste New wcs have horizontal branches which must be converted to fit the soil branch of the older 14° angle 'P' trap. wc pans should be connected to the cast-iron or plastic soil pipe with a flexible connector.

Ground-floor wcs, with the drain coming up from below, can be connected by pushing a finned pan-connector inside the clay pipe, thereby eliminating the need for a collar.

Slight misalignments between the soil pipe and the pan can often be overcome by using an offset pan-connector or an adjustable bend based upon a ball and socket joint.

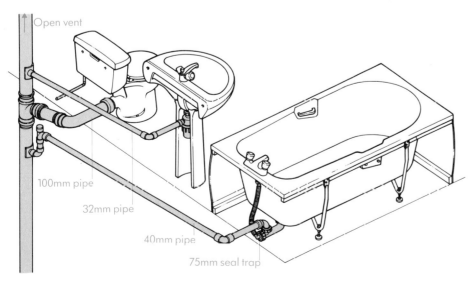

Open vent

100mm pipe

32mm pipe

40mm pipe

75mm seal trap

Left: The ideal arangement for waste pipes is short and straight. If bends are used, try to provide rodding access to clear blockages. Removable plastic traps are good as rodding access provided they can be got at.

REMOVING AN OLD SUITE

Breaking up a bath

1 Turn off the water supplying the taps and open them up to clear the pipes.

2 Turn on any ground-floor taps sharing the same supply-pipe to drain the residue.

3 Saw the pipes through just below the taps to disconnect them. It is only worth undoing them if the new bath is going in exactly the same position as the old one.

4 To break up a cast-iron bath you will need a sledge-hammer, a pair of stout gloves and ear and eye protectors (see illustration). Use sacking or an old towel to prevent flakes and chips from causing damage or injury.

Right: Undo the nut holding the flush pipe onto the cistern. Depending upon the materials used, a lubricant or joint-loosening solvent may prove helpful.

CHECKING THE FLOORBOARDS

With the bathroom suite out of the way, it is a good opportunity to examine the floorboards. Small, undetected leaks and spillages may have caused boards to rot. Check by digging a screwdriver blade into them. If they are soft or spongy they should be treated or replaced, depending upon how badly they have deteriorated. Remember that a full bath with a person in it can weigh 180kg (400lb) so the boards need to be good. If time allows, it is also worth treating the area around fitments with a timber treatment to guard against woodworm and rot.

Above: Clearing the room ready for the new suite means the job is finally underway. If there is building work and making good to do, cap off the pipe ends to stop debris falling down them. The new suite should be kept in another room until this stage is over.

Taking out a wc

1 Turn off the water and flush the cistern.

2 Disconnect the pipework using a wrench, and sponge out the remaining cistern water.

3 Remove the cistern by undoing fixing brackets or screws.

4 Stuff old cloths into the pan to displace the water and undo the floor screws. This might not be possible if they are rusted, in which case you will probably have to break the pan.

5 If the pan is cemented into the drain collar, gently tap around the pan outgo with a hammer to break the china.

6 Stuff a large wad of rag into the pipe end to prevent smells coming up and pieces falling down.

7 Gently chip out the remaining china with a small cold chisel. The collar is not needed, so do not worry if it breaks.

Taking out a basin

1 Turn off the water and drain the pipes thoroughly by turning on other taps shared by the fitment.

2 Undo the pipes from the taps, or saw through them if they are no longer needed in that position.

3 Disconnect the trap, bearing in mind there is a little water still in it.

4 Wall retaining screws or brackets underneath the basin might need undoing before you can remove it.

FITTING A BATH

Assemble the bath in a spacious area, preferably on carpet so you can lay it upside down.

1 Fit the frame first, then the waste and finally the taps and hand grips if supplied.

2 Screw the trap to the waste and the flexi connectors with the fibre washers to the taps.

3 Level it in place. This is done along the top edge with a spirit level. There is no need to worry about a slope to the waste – it is built in.

4 Mark out the positions of the waste-pipe connection to the trap and the two supply-pipe connections.

5 Draw a line on the wall along the top edge of the bath and remove the bath from the room.

6 Measure down from the line to create a channel of the same width as the bath edge.

7 Gently cut away the plaster line along the channel so the bath can be slightly let into the wall.

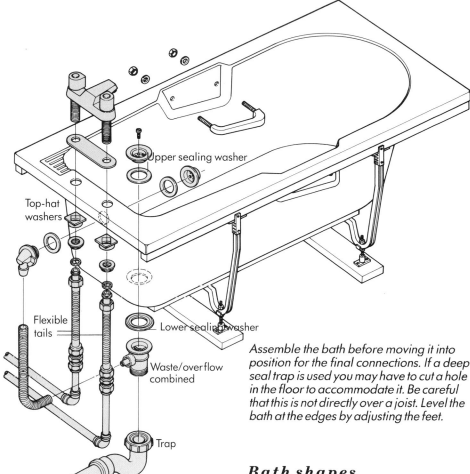

Upper sealing washer

Top-hat washers

Flexible tails

Lower sealing washer

Waste/overflow combined

Trap

Assemble the bath before moving it into position for the final connections. If a deep seal trap is used you may have to cut a hole in the floor to accommodate it. Be careful that this is not directly over a joist. Level the bath at the edges by adjusting the feet.

EXTRA SUPPORT

It is a good idea to screw a batten to the wall along the lower edge of the letting-in channel. This helps prevent movement and gives extra support to the edge frame.

Fit the waste and overflow, with the large rubber washers on the undersides, and the thin ones inside the bath. If this produces a lip around the plug hole, remove and seal on a bed of silicone.

Preparing the floor

Most baths have detailed instructions on how to fit the legs or cradles. Double-check all fixing screws to ensure that the frame will support the weight of the full bath.

Screw the feet on to timber bearers for added strength. This is essential on chipboard floors. The bearer must straddle the joists so it spreads the load over a larger area.

Connecting up to plumbing

1 Using flexi connectors it is often possible to tighten the supply joints before the bath is pushed into position. This saves having to use special spanners and a lot of frustration trying to reach up behind the bath. The connections are usually 22-mm compression joints, but if plain end connectors are used push-fit joints can be fitted making the job even easier.

2 Push the waste-pipe into the trap end and connect it up to the remaining run.

3 The bath is now ready for testing. Begin by running cold water through it and examining the waste run, then put in the plug and fill up to the overflow pipe. Pull the plug and test the waste again. Finally, fill the bath and make final adjustments to the feet and mark out the wall brackets.

Bath shapes

Many weird and wonderful baths are now available. Even though they appear very different from the traditional bath there is nothing in their fitting that differs greatly from the details shown here. Some corner baths with taps at the back require plumbing to be brought round the bath to accessible connection points, but with flexible plastic pipe even this once difficult task is now greatly simplified. It is also advisable to fit battens right into the corner, to prevent the back edge sagging and collecting water.

Above: *Acrylic and fibreglass baths are no longer the same old shape.*

FITTING A BASIN

Assembling the basin

Make sure you have all the clips and brackets to secure the basin firmly so it does not rely on the plumbing to hold it in position.

1 Fit the slotted waste with the rubber washer supplied, or silicone mastic, under the metal flange. The slots should line up approximately with the integral overflow. Tighten the backnut gently on to the washer.

2 Insert the single taps in their holes as shown in the illustration with an antirotation washer above the china and a plastic nut below. Use flexible connectors bent gently by thumbing round so they follow the line of the basin. Single-hole mixer taps have protective washers above and below the china.

Pedestal basins Try the basin on its pedestal against the wall for level. If the floor is out of level, pack one side of the pedestal up on a piece of vinyl tile. Mark screw-fixing holes and remove the basin to drill and plug holes. Never drill through the basin-fixing holes. Fit rubber washers under the screwheads.

Wall-hung basins These need good fixing points. A wood panel let in to the plaster can be screwed in several places to spread the weight.

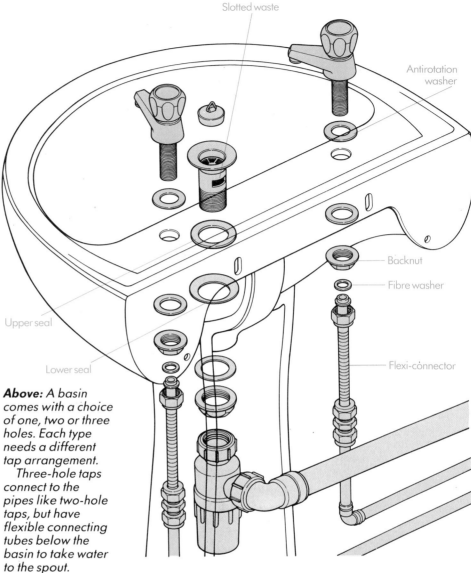

Above: A basin comes with a choice of one, two or three holes. Each type needs a different tap arrangement.
    Three-hole taps connect to the pipes like two-hole taps, but have flexible connecting tubes below the basin to take water to the spout.

Right: Plumbing, for a china inset basin, is the same, but the unit allows you to be a bit less fussy about where the pipes go. Thin acrylic basins have sink-type overflows. (Page 62 shows relevant details.)

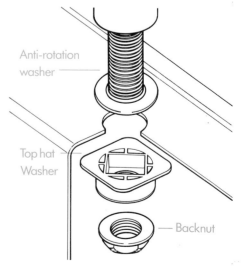

Above: Fit the tap with an antirotation washer on the upper side. A ½-in top hat washer can be used on the underside to give the nut a broader holding area and further reduce movement.

FITTING A WC

1 Position the pan first and select a connector to suit the soil pipe size and position. Use silicone lubricant if it is tight. It also helps to dip the connector in warm water.

2 Level the pan. On concrete floors use weak cement, on wooden floors use packing.

3 Mark out the floor-fixing holes, remove the pan and drill and plug for No. 12 screws. Refit the pan and draw a centre line up the wall.

4 Fix the cistern within the recommended height, making it level and central over the line.

5 Trial-fit the flush pipe and trim it to suit (within manufacturer's limits) with a junior hacksaw. Slip the flush nut over the flush pipe and fit the flush cone in the pan. If the flush pipe cannot be manoeuvred into both ends, undo the siphon nut and raise the siphon.

6 With the flush pipe pushed into the pan cone lower the siphon on to the pipe.

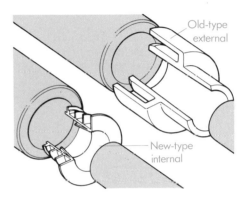

Two soft washers protect the china from the metal washers and wing nuts, which must be tightened by hand only. The fully-assembled unit is unstable until fixed against the wall with two rust proof screws and cushioning washers not supplied (use ¾-in tap washers). Fix the pan with rustproof screws in plastic cups to protect the china from the heads.

Water supply A small service-valve should be fitted in the pipe just before the swivel tap connector, to

The cistern is packed as a kit. Fit the flush siphon and lever arm mechanism on the same side as the ballvalve inlet to allow the float to operate. Choose the side that suits you. The overflow pipe goes in the remaining hole. Use the rubber washers on the inside of the cistern.

Above: *Two types of flush cone are used to join the pipe to the pan depending on the age of the fitment.*

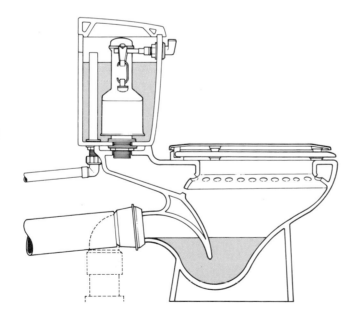

Right: *The close-coupled cistern is more compact, making it ideal below a window.*
The pan is a fixed distance from the wall, which might mean cutting back the soil branch or packing out the cistern back.

Above: *a modern Edwardian-style* wc *system and bidet.*

Close-coupled cistern Assemble the close-coupled cistern, as for the higher model, except for the addition of a metal plate which fits under the siphon nut. This holds two bolts which pull the cistern down on to a large 'doughnut' washer that fits around the flush nut and the seal between the pan and cistern.

provide a quick and easy method of turning off the water for rewashering or any other maintenance work that might be needed.

A choice of small seating for mains pressure and larger seating for tank-fed supplies is provided with the valve. Avoid overtightening the nut on to the ballvalve

thread as it is easily damaged.

The overflow pipe simply pushes up into the nut and socket and, once tightened, forms a low-pressure seal.

FITTING A SHOWER

Existing plumbing

If the shower is fed from your existing plumbing system and has other taps on the line it should be thermostatically controlled to maintain the temperature when the other taps are used.

A manual shower must have a separate cold supply fed from the tank so you cannot be scalded by a drop in cold pressure. The hot can be shared with other taps but a drop in temperature will occur when other hot taps are used.

Head pressure The cold tank height should be at least 1m (3ft) above the shower spray head to give an adequate pressure. (See the system diagram on page 11.) If this cannot be achieved, consider fitting a pump. On non-pumped showers, keep the supply pipes as short and straight as possible. On long pipe runs step up the pipe size to 22mm for the majority of the run. Avoid using elbows if the pipe can be gently bent.

Plastic pipe is ideal for supplying showers as it can often be run in one length. Use gate valves rather than stopcocks for isolating the supplies.

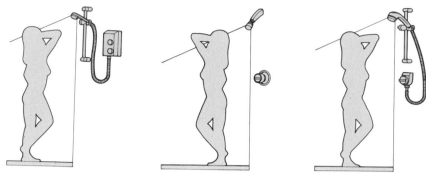

Shower types: instantaneous electric; and flush and surface thermostatic mixers.

Bath-mounted shower mixer

This is the simplest and the easiest to install, provided there is no problem with removing old taps.

The mixer tap is plumbed in on the tank-fed supplies (never the mains) and the flexible hose simply attaches to a wall-mounted bracket above the centre line of the bath. For safety, the cold supply must be fed as described above for a manual shower, unless a special thermostatic bath shower mixer is fitted.

Bath-mounted shower mixers can be thermostatically controlled.

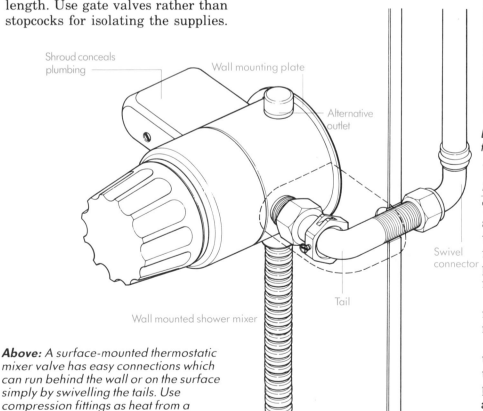

Shroud conceals plumbing

Wall mounting plate

Alternative outlet

Swivel connector

Tail

Wall mounted shower mixer

Above: *A surface-mounted thermostatic mixer valve has easy connections which can run behind the wall or on the surface simply by swivelling the tails. Use compression fittings as heat from a blowlamp will damage the valve.*

Wall-mounted shower mixer

This can be fed from surface-run supplies but is often brought through the wall or buried in channels cut in the brickwork. Plastic pipe is easiest, because it does not require corrosion protection.

Some showers have push-fit connectors but most need fitting with female iron-to-copper connectors.

Wrap PTFE tape around the threads. Screw the connectors on so that they face to meet the incoming pipes. When making connections, avoid using sealants which can block the mechanism.

Pumped showers

An electrically powered pump can be fitted to a shower either before the mixing valve (twin-impeller type) or after the valve (single-impeller type). It depends upon which one suits your plumbing system better.

To reduce noise, it is best to make the connections to the pump with plastic piping or flexible connectors.

The pump must be placed on, or near, floor level so that it is never run dry – a few seconds of dry running can ruin the bearings.

So long as the shower head is below the level of the water tank, automatic flow switches will turn on the electricity when the mixing valve is operated. If the shower is above the tank level (negative head) a separate switch will be needed. This is usually a low-voltage switch, fitted to the mixing valve control by the manufacturers as part of the negative head kit. The electrical supply to the pump is fed by twin and earth cable from a fused spur outlet outside the bathroom. In normal use it can be left switched on.

Right: A shower pump must be concealed away from the user of the shower so that the electrical parts cannot be touched accidentally. The space under a bath is ideal if it is panelled in afterwards but remember to make panels easily removable.

Single-impeller pumps The connections to the mixing valve are made in the usual way – hot and cold are mixed before reaching the pump. The mixed supply is then taken down to the floor-mounted pump and back up to the spray head.

Twin-impeller pumps The cold comes from the tank and the hot connection is taken from near the cylinder on the vent pipe. Some manufacturers recommend fitting an Essex flange into the cylinder wall to give an independent hot supply and also to stop air being sucked down the cylinder vent pipe by the action of the pump. Air drawn into the pump will also cause spluttering and fluctuating temperature at the shower head.

The Essex flange comes with complete instructions; the only special tool required is a hole cutter. If you have a cylinder with a brass plug in the side near the top, this can be removed and the tapping used for the shower pump.

To make any connection to the cylinder itself you will need to turn off the cold feed and drain down by attaching a hosepipe to the small draincock at the bottom. Make sure the immersion heater is in the off position. Run the hose to a lower drain and open the small square spindle head. Make the connection to the cylinder and run a short piece of pipe out to a gate valve.

If the connection is made on the vent pipe, simply turn off.

Head height

Essex flange

Twin-impeller pump

Above: A few inches head (indicated by arrow) is needed to start the pump automatically.

ELECTRIC SHOWERS

The water

The advantage of an electric shower is that the mains-fed plumbing allows it to go anywhere. Once again, plastic pipe lends itself to the job since it can be buried in walls, run through the loft or ducting, and generally threaded through small spaces, including round the back of the bath.

The connection to the mains can be made first or last. Tee into the mains water by turning off the water and cutting the pipe. Use a compression fitting for speed and ease, and fit an isolating valve on the branch. The mains water can then be restored to the rest of the house, leaving you to complete the plumbing at a much more leisurely pace.

Electrics

It should be accepted that the information here cannot provide a comprehensive instruction to a person inexperienced in electrical work. If you are not confident about your ability to carry out this part of the job safely, leave it to a plumbing professional.

The shower must always be supplied by a twin and earth cable of at least 6mm². Use 10mm² if the length is over 23m (75ft). A separate spare fuseway must be used here to connect the cable at the fusebox.

It is strongly recommended that an RCD circuit-breaker is incorporated in the supply to give added protection to the user.

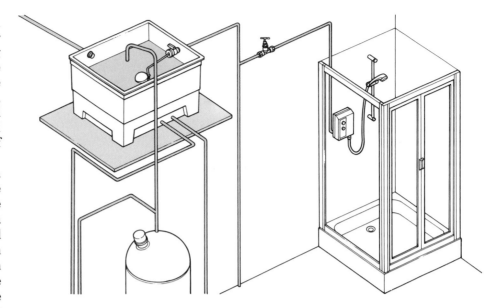

The earth wire is the most important connection in the installation. In addition to the one in the appliance, a separate earth must be connected to the pipework.

All metal pipework in the house must be earthed. Use a special adjustable band around each pipe and run earth cable from band to band. The cable must run all the way back to the main earth terminal near the consumer unit.

With the electricity turned off at the mains, connect the red live wire of the supply cable into the top of the fuseway in the consumer unit. Sleeve the earth and connect to the common earth terminal. The black neutral must join the other neutrals on the common neutral terminal.

Electric showers are simple to plumb in. Take the water supply from the nearest convenient point on the rising main, via an isolating valve, to the inlet union on the shower unit.

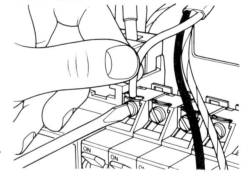

Connect the red cable core to its own 30A fuseway in the consumer unit, next to other similar fuses.

Shower end connections Mount the shower box on the wall. Connect the cable to the terminals marked LNE in the shower, passing it through the rubber grommet and under the restraining bar. Fit the connector elbow to the shower inlet with a fibre washer or compression ring, and point it towards the pipe entry. Flush the pipework through before making the final connection.

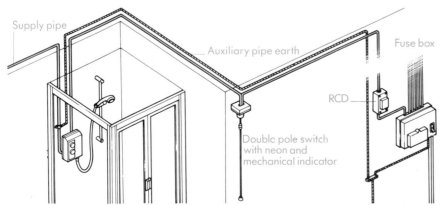

Earth continuity bonding is a safety requirement. It ensures that, if a fault develops, the current passes through the earth cable and not through you.

SHOWER TRAYS AND CUBICLES

The floor

A shower tray must have a firm floor to rest on in order to avoid movement. If the floor is chipboard, screw a piece of 13-mm (½-in) plywood on the floor. The floor should be level; if it is not, choose a tray with adjustable feet and side panels. This also makes clearing the trap easier.

Right: A free-standing ready-plumbed shower cubicle takes only a few hours to fit and is ready for use immediately. It can also be moved to another room later if required.

Left and above: There is no need to stick to the conventional square shaped shower tray. There are now a number of different designs, but bear in mind that the cubicle may also have to be adapated or even specially made.

The wall

Most trays have slightly tapering sides, which means they do not sit right against the wall at their top edge. To get a better fit, chop out plaster and set the tray in slightly. The wall tiles can then come down on top of the tray – not behind.

Levelling

On models with no feet, you might have to cut a hole in the floor to let the trap sit below the boards. You will also need to provide a screwed-down access hatch beside the tray to reach the trap. Do not position the tray with the waste hole next to the wall if there is no access to the trap.

Cubicles

These come as assembly kits and usually need nothing more than a screwdriver, a drill and a spirit level to put together. Measure the tray size at the top edge and purchase a cubicle to fit that size. Check whether the walls are upright; if they are not, make sure your cubicle includes profiles which allow for this. Work out which way the door will open and check it has enough clearance. If the profiles are being fitted to plasterboard, use special fixing plugs.

Seal the plasterboard before tiling with waterproof tile adhesive.

Cover the tray with a heavy blanket when tiling, as a tile dropped on its corner can break the tray.

Seal the joint between the tiles and tray with silicone sealant or a plastic quadrant that goes under the tiles and over the tray.

BIDETS

Types of bidet

Overrim fill The overrim fill bidet is the easiest of the two types of bidet to install but it does not have the ascending spray or rim-fill facilities most people associate with a bidet.

The plumbing connections are the same as for a basin in every respect, except that they are lower down – so there is not quite so much room to play with.

This is likely to be more critical with the 32-mm (1¼-in) trap and waste-pipe than with the supplies. Aim to conceal all the pipework behind the china horseshoe at the back. The 15-mm (⅝-in) supplies can be run in copper or flexible plastic to points directly below the taps, leaving the final connections to be made with flexi connectors.

Ascending spray

An ascending spray bidet has a more complicated pop-up waste and diverter valve mechanism, sending water through the china (porcelain) to discharge around the rim. This arrangement has the potential to contaminate water to other fitments unless the water by-laws are followed.

All the seals and hoses are supplied with the taps as a kit and, provided they are fitted in order, this part of the job is logical assembly. Avoid force when doing up nuts – a little past hand-tight, just to compress the rubber slightly, should be enough.

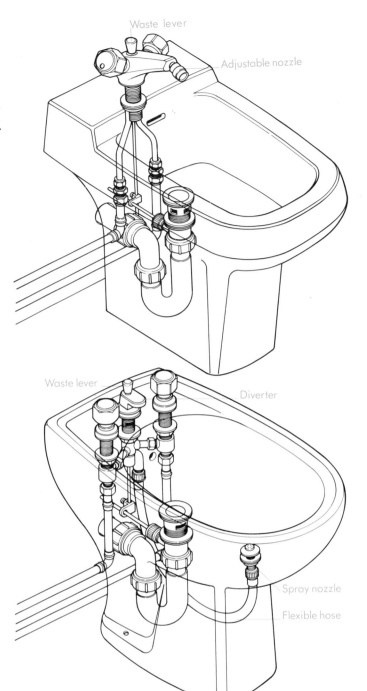

Waste lever
Adjustable nozzle

Left: *Overrim-fill bidets do not require any special plumbing arrangements. They often use basin taps and are straightforward to fit.*

Waste lever
Diverter

Left: *Ascending spray bidets are a lot more complicated and require careful plumbing in to avoid contamination of other water supplies. The spray height has an adjusting screw.*

Spray nozzle
Flexible hose

Below: *There are regulations to observe when installing an ascending spray bidet.*

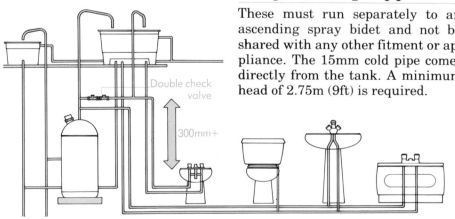

Double check valve
300mm+

The plumbing supplies

These must run separately to an ascending spray bidet and not be shared with any other fitment or appliance. The 15mm cold pipe comes directly from the tank. A minimum head of 2.75m (9ft) is required.

Hot water This is taken from a branch off the cylinder vent pipe at least 300mm (12in) above the bidet rim. The supply must then run through a non-return valve (double-check valve) of at least the same height, to prevent it returning to the system from beyond this point. As an extra precaution, an air break, in the form of an extra vent pipe, is required immediately after the check valve. Local by-laws may allow this to be an air inlet valve instead of a pipe, but confirm this with the local water authority first.

CONCEALING BATHROOM PIPES

Leaving access to pipes

Boxed-in or panelled-over pipework must be left with access in case leaks occur. Whole tile sections can be mounted on plywood and fixed with ball catches, or individual panels can be screwed through screw cups.

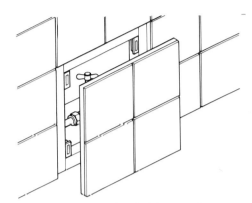

Above: *Magnetic clips hold a panel.*

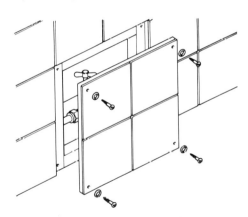

Above: *Screw cups are neat and easy.*

Where a waste pipe passes through an outside wall and is working satisfactorily fill the surrounding hole with a weak mortar mix and finish it flush with the brickwork.

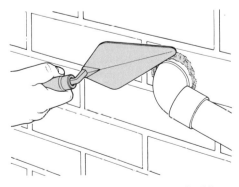

Above: *Avoid too strong a mortar for filling.*

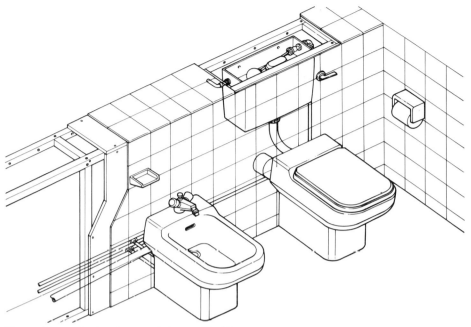

Above: *Not a single pipe need show with this arrangement.*

Timber and tiles

Stout 50mm × 50mm (2 in × 2 in) or larger framework should be glued and screwed behind plywood panels which are to be tiled over in order to increase rigidity. Movement and vibration, caused by slamming doors and so on can cause tiles to fall off, possibly damaging the bathroom suite.

Prime timber, plasterboard or chipboard with paint or PVA adhesive and use flexible tile adhesive to allow for slight movement.

A streamlined bathroom is ideal if space is limited. Back-to-the-wall WCs and concealed cisterns are ideal for this. The flush handle assembly is adjustable to fit various wall thicknesses. The top of the cistern should be accessible through a removable cover for ballvalve rewashering and adjustment. Insulation inside the boxwork will reduce noises. Pipework and cables can run unseen.

A mistake when making good around pipework is using too strong a mix, causing it to crack. Sand and cement should not be more than 1 part cement to 4½ parts of sand.

Allowing for expansion

Sleeve the supply pipework through walls with insulation or plastic.

Alternatively, urethane filler foam insulates and protects against damage and can be plastered over.

Where pipework runs across joists a single turn of felt lagging will prevent expansion noises.

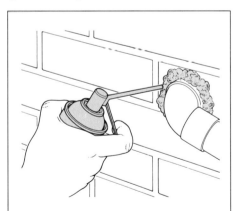

FILLING IN WASTE HOLES

Fill all waste holes to the outside as soon as you can – even if it is only a temporary arrangement – with polythene bags. Many a vermin infestation has begun with rats or mice entering through holes and gaps left by plumbers, and once they are in, it can be difficult to get rid of them.

FITTING A KITCHEN SINK

Whether swapping over a sink in the same position or fitting a totally new kitchen, one of the most important tools you will need is a tape measure. With sinks coming in so many shapes and sizes, you need to make certain that the model you have chosen is right for the location. If it is part of a new kitchen, think about the distances between the cooker, sink and fridge.

The plumbing supplies for any sink are the same up to the point where they connect to the taps and waste; and here they vary a great deal. Fortunately, there are now waste kits available, which make the job a lot easier than trying to marry up individual components. This plumbing can also be utilized to plumb in a dishwasher or washing machine – the connections are almost identical. Labour-saving quick-fit devices for taking water both in and out mean that the kitchen can soon be in full working order.

SIT-ON SINKS

Fit the waste and overflow on to the sink using the seals provided. If you have the older banjo type you will need silicone sealant and back washers. Do not use putty: it attacks the plastic. Even a small leak, if undetected, can damage the base unit.

Fit the taps with a rubber seal between the underside of the tap body and the sink. On two-hole mixers and single-hole pillar taps you will need a pair of ½-in top hat washers to act as spacers between the nut and sink.

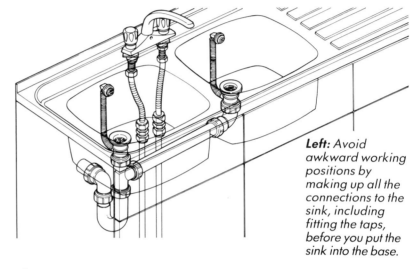

Left: Avoid awkward working positions by making up all the connections to the sink, including fitting the taps, before you put the sink into the base.

Check that the arm reach of the tap is right for the sinks. Too short an arm makes filling a kettle difficult.

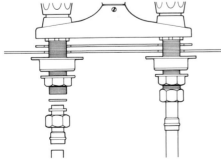

Above: Top hat washers are essential to pull the tap down on to its rubber seal.

Connecting up

Not forgetting to insert fibre washers on the tap connector flanges, attach two flexible tails or straight runs of pipe to the taps, in order to bring the connections below the level of the bowl when the sink is fitted. This avoids the need to use special basin wrenches to reach them when you connect up the rest of the pipework. Sit the sink on the base unit and measure the position of the trap-to-waste-pipe connection. If the waste-pipe is going directly out through the wall, allow approximately a 13-mm (½-in) fall from the trap and mark the centre for the hole. Remove the sink and cut the hole in the wall, either by hiring a 50-mm (2-in) core bit, or using a hammer and cold chisel. It helps to drill a hole all the way through so that you can cut from both sides.

Refit the sink with the retaining clips tightened in position, connect the incoming 15-mm pipes to the tails and fit the 40-mm (1½-in) waste-pipe to the trap.

Base units As modern base units are made for a variety of sinks and worktops you will need to check that yours is suitable for the sink you have chosen.

If drawer fronts are supplied these must be the dummy type which simply screw on the front of the unit with concealed brackets. A drawer next to a sink bowl is possible if there is sufficient clearance but sometimes this is tight so check the measurements first. If in doubt ask the salesperson to confirm the suitability.

Back rails are also a problem because they are often in the way of the tap connectors. By using flexible tap connectors the tails can usually be bent around any obstruction but even then a limited amount of cutting of the back rail might be required. You might also have to cut the shelf slightly to accommodate the trap.

It is a good idea to leave the doors off the unit until the plumbing has been completed and tested.

INSET SINKS

Cutting the hole

First, fix the worktop on the units so the position of the sink can be marked in relation to the front rail and the unit sides. Many sinks do not leave much room, particularly if the taps are being mounted in the worktop behind the sink. Remember – measure twice; cut once.

Use the template provided or the upturned sink to draw the outline on the worktop. Make sure the front line is parallel with the edge of the worktop. The template provides the cutting line, but if you used the sink draw an inner line for cutting.

Drill a hole within the cutting line and use an electric jigsaw to cut slowly around. Apply only gentle forward pressure to avoid wandering from the cutting line. Clamp a batten along straight cuts to coincide with the edge of the saw's soleplate as a cutting guide. Prop the underside with a couple of pieces of wood (not your hands) to stop it falling.

Connecting up

Fit the waste kit and the taps before putting the sink back in the cutout. Waste kits often need their connecting pipes trimmed to adjust to the distance between the bowls. Bear in mind the intended position of the trap-to-waste-pipe connection. There must be no backfall to the sink on the pipe, or blockages may occur. If a waste disposal unit is not being fitted, a basket strainer waste can be used in its place.

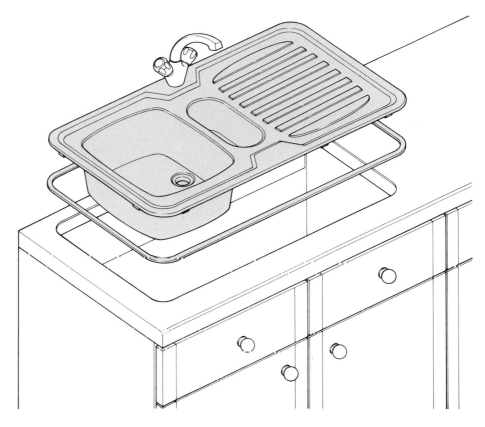

Above: *The sink is pulled down on to a strip of flexible sealant by clips attached to the underside. Tighten the clips gently, working your way round twice to compress the sealant evenly.*

Monoblock mixers. The modern single-hole monoblock tap mixer has one large back nut. If the tap is fitted directly onto a thin section steel sink it will require some bracing on the underside. Some taps include a plate for this purpose but if one is not supplied use a large top-hat washer or make a plate from a piece of metal. The tails should be left straight until the plate and nut are threaded on, then gently bent to suit the plumbing. Avoid overbending them as it is possible to kink the copper.

If the sink has no hole and no provision for drilling one (as with some plastic sinks) the hole must be made in the worktop behind the sink. An allowance must be made for this when positioning the sink and you must also take care that the backnut is not fouled by the sink or the unit.

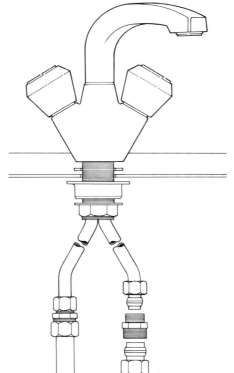

Monoblock flexible copper tap connector tails join to the supply pipes with compression fittings usually provided in the box.

SEALING THE HOLE

Try the sink in position and make any minor adjustments necessary to accommodate the clips. Remove the sink and paint the cut edge of the worktop with polyurethane varnish as a precaution against swelling.

Ordinary silicone bath sealant makes an excellent, long-lasting seal which can be used as a back-up around the very edge of the hole.

PLUMBING IN A WASHING MACHINE

The most convenient position for plumbing in a washing machine or dishwasher is next to or near the sink. This allows the supply and waste-pipes already serving the sink to be used for the machines. The detergent waste water from the machines also helps to keep the waste-pipe free from grease and smells.

If you want to place the machine elsewhere, such as in a utility room or even a cellar, the supplies and waste will have to be run from and to convenient points. The supply pipes can be run in 15-mm (⅝-in) copper or plastic and the waste-pipe in 40-mm (1½-in) plastic. Always consult the manufacturer's instructions.

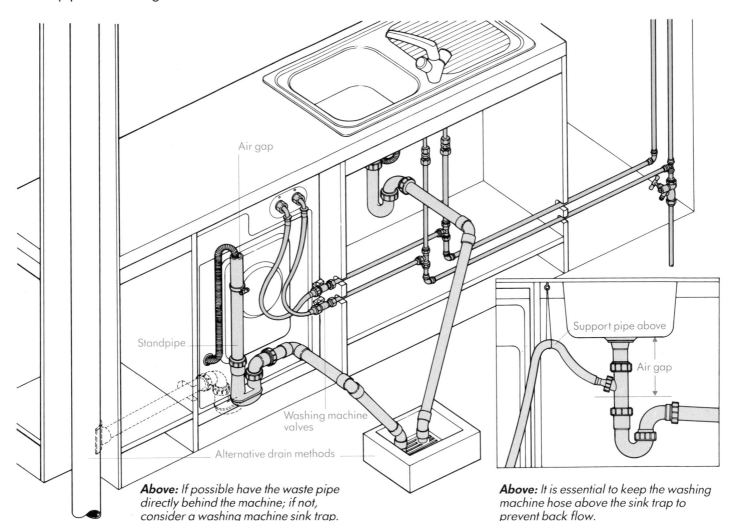

Above: If possible have the waste pipe directly behind the machine; if not, consider a washing machine sink trap.

Above: It is essential to keep the washing machine hose above the sink trap to prevent back flow.

A large variety of plumbing kits are available for both the supplies and waste to make the job quick and easy.

A dishwasher uses only one water supply hose, usually fed from the cold mains. A washing machine can have hot and cold, or cold only. If the machine has its own internal electric water heater (most do), you can use a 'Y' piece to feed both supplies from a single cold supply.

In addition, you will need a 13-amp socket outlet with an accessible switch.

The waste hose This must discharge higher than the top of the drum to prevent siphonage. It must also have an air gap or inlet at its uppermost point for the same purpose. A 40-mm (1½-in) standpipe with a low trap meets this requirement, as does a spigot that is above the standing water level of the trap.

A direct connection plumbing-out connector that clips on to the waste-pipe might need an additional vacuum breaker air inlet valve — check the manufacturer's instruction leaflet.

Supply pipes Sufficient pressure must be available to let water past the solenoid valves inside the machine.

In most homes the height of the cold tank is enough to provide the necessary water pressure, but in some flats with a water tank in the airing cupboard the pressure might be too low. Machine manufacturers will advise on low-pressure valves to overcome this problem, or both hot and cold can be supplied from the high-pressure cold mains and heated within the machine.

WATER IN

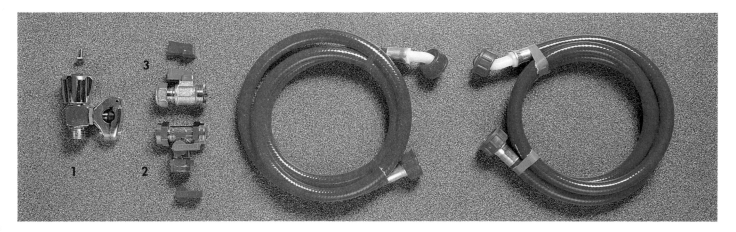

Above: 1. Self-tapping washing machine valve. 2. Washing machine slip tee. 3. Washing machine straight valve.

Lever-type valves These are specially made to go on the end of the supply pipes, to provide a quick means of shutting off the water. Their ¾-in threaded end is designed to connect the hoses directly. A rubber washer must be placed in the hose ends to make the seal between the valve end and hose.

Self-tapping Clamp-on washing machine valves can be used to provide connection points on existing pipe runs. It is not necessary to turn off the water to use these devices, but make sure you can. Secure the clamp to the pipe before screwing in the self-tapper. These fittings are not suitable for use on plastic pipes.

Slip tee valves With this type it is necessary to turn off the water and drain the pipe before cutting it. Cut out a piece of pipe about 13mm (½ in) long and slip on the compression nuts and rings. Move the pipe slightly out of line and slide on the tee. Position it centrally across the gap and tighten the nuts.

WATER OUT

Sink traps These can be substituted for a special washing machine trap (see below) which includes a spigot for connecting a washing machine or dishwasher. Make sure the hosepipe is fed in from above the trap so waste water from the sink does not flow backwards into the machine.

Standpipes These rise up from a trap, providing an independent washing machine waste, but if the waste-pipe is teed into an existing sink-waste run there is always the chance that a blockage will cause the standpipe to back up with water and overflow.

A standpipe is not recommended for anywhere other than ground-floor installations.

Self-tapping These clamp-on waste outlets are a quick and easy method of connecting into existing waste-pipes, but they must be at least near the top of the machine drum. Consult the machine manufacturer's instruction booklet to find out if the height is within their limits. Dishwasher outlets can be lower.

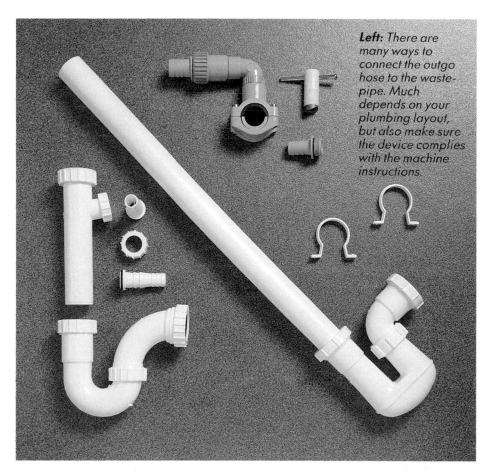

Left: There are many ways to connect the outgo hose to the waste-pipe. Much depends on your plumbing layout, but also make sure the device complies with the machine instructions.

PROJECTS AROUND THE HOME

Unlike the kitchen and bathroom, the plumbing around your home, particularly in the cupboards and loft (if you have one), is not likely to inspire change. Nobody gets rid of their old tank because they are fed up with the colour. Usually it is because that rust spot in the bottom is about to, or already has, produced a damp patch on the ceiling. An emergency repair might tide you over, but the real answer is a renewal.

Similarly, gutters and downpipes might drip, and even pour, before coming to your attention. (Who walks around the outside of their house in the pouring rain?)

The damage that can be caused by neglecting such things is often very costly. Not surprisingly, these types of plumbing faults are just the kind of problems picked up by building surveyors when properties are up for sale, so it obviously pays to keep an eye open.

FITTING A NEW WATER TANK

Remove the old tank by disconnecting or cutting back the pipework at a convenient point.

A round flexible tank can often be squeezed through a small loft hatch but if this is not possible use two smaller tanks and connect them with 28mm pipework low down. When using this arrangement make sure that the ballvalve inlet and the supply outlet are on different tanks to ensure a good flow of water through both tanks.

Build a strong wooden base for the tanks and make sure they are positioned over a wall to prevent the joists sagging. The ballvalve connection must be at least 25mm below the top of the tank and the overflow connection at least 25mm below that. The float is then adjusted to make sure the water level is at least 25mm below the overflow pipe.

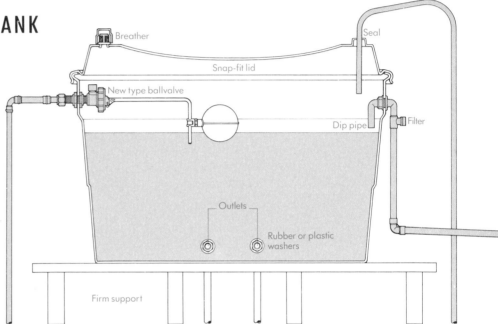

Above: *Drill the tank and fit all the connectors and the ballvalve before positioning it.*

By-laws

Additional requirements to guard against contamination of the water and frost damage are now in force.

Plastic tanks are flexible and can often be squeezed through small loft hatches, but take care – they can also be damaged by rough handling. Examine the tank for faults.

Unlike steel, plastic tanks need supporting evenly on a flat base, preferably with water-repellant boarding, not chipboard. If the tank is being repositioned in the loft, make sure the load (1 kilo per litre [10 lb per gallon]) is supported. A tank laid on the middle of 100mm × 50mm (4 in × 2 in) ceiling joists stands a chance of ending up in the bedroom.

Cut all holes in the tank with an electric drill and hole-saw attachment. The holes should provide snug fits for the connectors. Fit a bracing plate (supplied with the tank) to the outside of the ballvalve connection. Tighten the nuts to provide rigid support: this will prevent the tank from flexing when the ballvalve is shutting off.

The outlets must be at least 25mm clear of the bottom to prevent debris being drawn into the pipework. Tank connectors should have rubber washers and polypropelene washers each side. PTFE tape can be used around threads as an extra precaution against leaks.

Run the outlet pipework up to the connectors so that there is a continuous fall away from the tank to prevent air being trapped in high spots.

Connecting the pipes The ideal pipe for connecting up a new tank to existing pipework is flexible plastic because it can be gently bent to align with the connectors. It is fairly frost resistant but still needs insulating. Another advantage is that you will not have to use a blowlamp in the loft. Push-fit connectors make the job even easier and limit the number of tools you will need. One exception is the vent pipe, which must be metal. The lid has a hole for this and a rubber seal prevents insects crawling in.

Take the hook of the vent pipe at least 300mm above the tank and make sure the end terminates above the overflow level to allow it to draw air rather than water. All pipework to and from the tank must be well supported with clips.

FITTING A CYLINDER

When buying a new cylinder, think about whether you need a larger capacity. Indirect cylinders, which are common in modern installations, have a coil to keep the central heating water separate. A more simple direct cylinder is for use with an immersion heater or with a very old solid fuel boiler. If you heat water with an electric immersion but plan to add central heating in the future, an indirect cylinder can be fitted and the primary coil left open until it is needed.

SAFETY WARNING

Before carrying out any work, make sure you understand the principles of heating and the tank-fed system (explained on pages 11-14). If in doubt, seek professional advice.

How to do it

1 Try the cylinder in position first and work out the most convenient way to bring in the pipes. Turn the cylinder around to suit the boiler flow and return.

2 Loosely screw the fittings into their tappings on the cylinder and work out how to run pipes so they do not cross over. Try to avoid running pipes across the front of the cylinder, as this will involve a lot of work if you ever have to remove it.

3 Remove the fittings one by one and wrap the threads with PTFE tape before refitting with a wrench. Do not overtighten.

The cold feed This must have a draincock at its lowest point. If this is not accessible with the cylinder in position, run a 15-mm tee from the pipe and fit a draincock around the front of the cylinder.

If the water tank is lower than 2m (6ft) from the top of the cylinder, or if the demand is likely to be from several taps simultaneously, a 28-mm cold feed should be used. For tanks above this height a 22-mm pipe will provide enough pressure. If in doubt, fit the larger pipe.

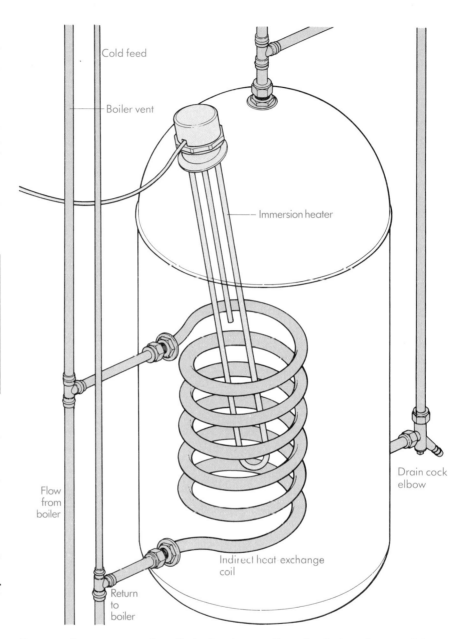

Cold feed

Boiler vent

Immersion heater

Flow from boiler

Return to boiler

Indirect heat exchange coil

Drain cock elbow

Connect what you can to the cylinder in advance. Keep the draincock accessible.

The vent connection This can be made in 22-mm if a 1-in threaded × 22-mm compression-reducing connector is used. If hot water demand is heavy, use a 1-in threaded BSP × 28-mm fitting and run the pipe to the taps in 28-mm. The vent pipe must rise continuously to its open end to prevent air locks.

The hot supply Insert a tee for the hot taps somewhere in the lower part of the vent pipe, so that the rest of the vent can be run in 22-mm even if the supply to the taps is 28-mm. Fill the cylinder from the tank and test it.

Boiler connections Use 1-in female threaded brass fittings or purpose-made cylinder unions with fibre washers and run from the primary coil down to the boiler.

1 Wrap PTFE tape around the protruding (male) threads and screw on either straight or angled fittings.

2 Fit a short pipe into the top connection and run a tee upstand on the other end either up to the open vent above the feed and expansion tank, or to an aircock 30mm (12in) or so above the flow. This will release air trapped in the top of the coil.

FITTING AN IMMERSION HEATER

An immersion heater can be used to supply all your hot water or as an emergency back-up if the boiler breaks down. By using a time switch, set to come on during off-peak electricity rates, an immersion heater can work out a lot cheaper than running a boiler during the summer just to heat tap water.

Because fitting a heater involves both plumbing and electrical work, having the job done professionally can often mean calling in two tradesmen; so, doing the whole job yourself is therefore a double money saver. If you prefer, you can of course leave the electrics to a professional and just carry out the plumbing.

Cylinders now come with an immersion heater tapping-hole which must be sealed either by an immersion heater or a blanking plug. An immersion heater is a useful back-up, a blanking plug merely fills the hole.

Fitting an immersion heater could mean changing a burnt-out heater, fitting one in a new cylinder or putting one in an old cylinder which has a blanking plate.

If the cylinder is full of water, start from Draining down. If the cylinder is new, start from Screwing in the element.

Draining down

1 Turn off the cold feed from the tank and turn on a hot tap.
2 Attach a garden hosepipe to the draincock at the bottom of the cylinder and unscrew the square-headed spindle with a pair of grips. Drain off a couple of gallons of water. (You need not drain it all away.)
3 Unscrew the blanking plate in the top with the special immersion heater spanner, which can be hired. Do not use large grips or you might damage the cylinder.

Screwing in the element

1 Thread the large fibre ring over the heater element and carefully place the heater into the boss. The element fits down inside the indirect coil, but it can be difficult to get it perfectly aligned.
2 When it is correctly positioned the heater will screw round by hand; if it will not, it has been cross-threaded.
3 Tighten the heater with the spanner, but do not worry about a final tightening until the cylinder is filled.
4 Turn off the hot tap, turn on the cold feed and the cylinder will fill.
5 If there is any seepage, give the heater a further small turn.

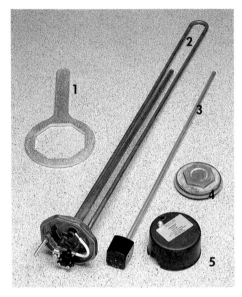

LOOSENING THE BOSS

If the cylinder boss or old heater is stuck, use a gentle blowlamp flame to warm it up. Try again while it is hot. When the hole is clear, clean the top around the flange with some steel wool.

Left:
1: Immersion heater spanner
2: Immersion heater
3: Dry pocket thermostat
4: Blanking plug
5: Protective cap

Below: Use a length of 1.5mm² (minimum) butyl rubber heat-resistant flex to connect the heater to the switch outlet. The flex must go via a thermostat within the heater. This should be adjusted to between 60 and 65° centigrade. The 2.5mm² supply cable to the connection point must connect to the fuse box on its own 15 amp fuseway.

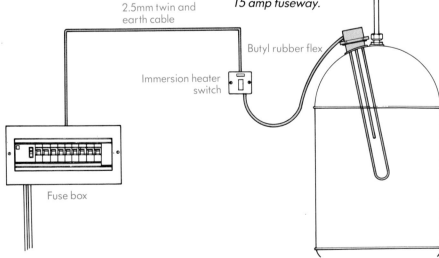

2.5mm twin and earth cable

Immersion heater switch

Butyl rubber flex

Fuse box

FITTING AN OUTSIDE TAP

Choosing a location

An outside tap complete with a hosepipe nozzle can be fitted using a kit or separate components, but before buying any parts decide which is the most suitable location for your tap. Ideally, the tap should be above a drain to take away any spillages, but if this is not possible an area of hard standing that slopes away from the house will do.

Try to choose a position that is conveniently close to internal mains water plumbing. Outside, just under the position of the kitchen sink is a good spot.

A long drill bit can be hired to make the hole through the wall. A 22-mm bit will allow a length of ¾-in plastic overflow to be passed through as a sleeve. This not only protects the pipe but makes sure no leaks go undetected inside the wall.

Wherever practicable, make sure that outside pipework faces down to the tap so residual water can be drained in winter. All outside pipework should be as short as possible.

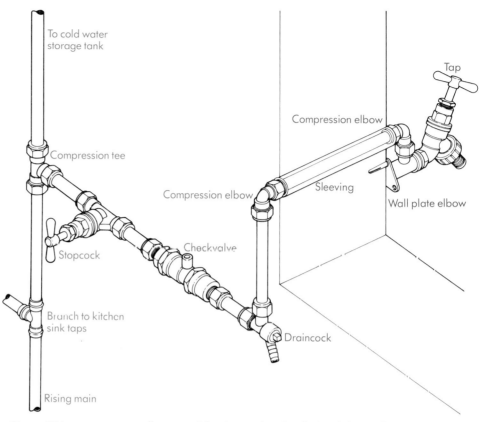

Above: *This arrangement allows outside pipework to be drained during the winter.*

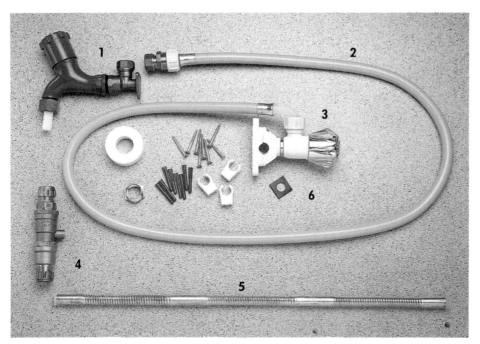

Above: *An outside tap kit. Apart from the normal plumbing tools used for cutting and joining pipe, you will also need to hire a long masonry drill bit and possibly an electric drill, if your own is too small. Sleeving is not included.*

1: Hose union bib tap
2: Flexible hose (plastic)
3: Self-tapping isolating valve
4: Double seal check valve
5: Flexible pipe (copper)
6: Rubber sealing washer

How to do it

1 Turn off the rising main and drain the water through the kitchen tap.
2 Mark and cut the pipe to insert a tee at a convenient point. If there is no give on the pipe to get an ordinary tee in, use a slip tee which has no internal stops. Position it accurately over the gap in the pipe.
3 Fit a stopcock to the pipe with the arrow stamped on the body pointing in the direction of the flow.
4 Fit an approved double-seal check valve, then an inline draincock.
5 Run the pipe through the wall sleeve. On the outside turn one male/female elbow straight from the pipe passing through the wall into the backplate elbow. This does away with any outside pipework.
6 Mark, drill and plug the holes for the backplate elbow, then screw it to the wall with a minimum of 32-mm (1¼-in) brass screws. Seal the tap into the elbow with PTFE tape wrapped around the thread and/or a fibre washer over the thread.

REPLACING RAINWATER GUTTERING AND DOWNPIPES

Safe working

Cast-iron gutter is heavy and awkward to remove. The sudden weight as you take it from the brackets can easily topple you off a ladder.

If there is room, it is safer to work from a quick tower scaffold, which can be hired. Where space is restricted, use a ladder with a stay to keep you above and in front of the gutter, rather than below it. Tie the ladder to eye bolts screwed into the fascia board. Use barriers and warnings to keep people from the area while you are taking the gutter down. Do not have a helper down below for this part of the job, in case something falls.

Removing the old gutter

- Unscrew or lever off the old gutter brackets and remove short sections of gutter. If it does not break at the joins, tap it gently with a hammer. Wear eye protection in case bits fly.
- Brush off the loose paint. Apply two coats of quick-drying paint to the exposed woodwork.

Deciding the levels Gutters should not fall too steeply, or rain will be blown behind them to rot the fascia board. A slight fall of 1 in 300 is usually sufficient, unless there are too few outlets for the length of the runs. Start the gutter with its highest bracket up under the tile.

Fixing the brackets Use a spirit level to draw two marks at the opposite ends of each fascia board. Work out the required fall to the downpipe and screw the outlet to the fascia.

Screw another bracket to the fascia at the other end, using the level line as your reference point for setting this bracket higher. Take a string line and tie it around the bracket where the gutter will sit. Stretch the line to the other bracket and tie it tautly in the exact same point on the other bracket. Screw all the other brackets and joining pieces to the fascia at 1-m (3-ft) intervals, using this line as a guide. Do not let them push the line up.

FITTING GUTTERS

All joins, corners and outlets are marked inside with a line to which the gutter is fixed. This allows for expansion of the gutter within the bracket. If the gutter is fixed beyond this line it will creak and twist in the sun, possibly breaking a bracket.

If the gutter is being fixed in very hot weather it should be stored in the shade before fixing so that it is not already expanded. Cut the gutter with a fine tooth saw, using a spare bracket as a guide, then remove rough edges before using.

Joining to cast-iron

Plastic gutter can be joined to cast-iron using a special bracket adaptor.

Drill a hole in the gutter, if one does not exist, to take a mushroom-headed gutter bolt. Use a tube of rubberized mastic gutter sealant to make the joint.

Use rustproof, fast thread, No. 10 roundhead screws to fix the brackets. They are easier to drive in, especially when working one-handed from a ladder. The screws must go into the wood by at least 19mm (¾in) to withstand snow loads.

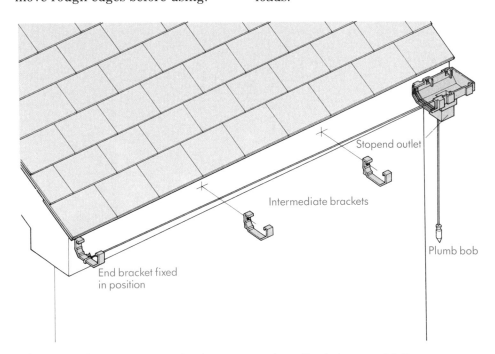

Above: Brackets are positioned with a taut string line. Check the overall fall is correct before you begin fixing them into the fascia.

Above: A ladderseat makes it easier.

Fitting gutter into joints If the ends have been cut, make sure they are square and free of burrs. Engage the back edge of the gutter under the lip and flex the front in. You will hear a click as it engages. In cold weather, the gutter ends will be more difficult to engage. Store them indoors just before using to improve their malleability.

Fitting gutter into brackets Work your way along the gutter, engaging first the back edge and then the front by sharply pulling it down until it clicks under the bracket.

FITTING DOWNPIPES

Cast-iron downpipes tend to outlast gutters, so it is not always necessary to replace them at the same time as the gutter. However, they might look better than they are because corrosion takes place along the back, while the front, which benefits from frequent coats of paint, can look pristine. Feel up and down the back with your fingers for holes or thin areas. Also examine the pipes and joints for cracks caused by frost.

Removing old pipes

Start from the bottom and work up. Use a crowbar or similar lever to ease forward the lugs on the pipe socket. A piece of wood placed behind the lever will help prevent damage to the brickwork.

Once the nail head has been pulled forward it can be eased out with the crowbar.

Fitting the new downpipes

Hang a plumbline on a long nail from the top of the wall so that it falls over the drain gully. Mark a series of chalk lines exactly behind the line to give a perfectly vertical reference point.

Remove the line and, using a downpipe bracket centred on the chalk line, mark the holes for the first bracket. Measure the distance of the holes from the line and mark the holes for the remaining brackets at a maximum of 2m (6 ft) apart.

1 Fit the lowest bracket around the shoe unless the pipe is going straight into a gulley cover plate. Place the first run of pipe in the shoe and screw the remaining brackets to the wall.
2 Place the lower half of the socket inside the bottom pipe ready for the upper pipe to be inserted into the socket. Allow for expansion by withdrawing the pipe 6mm (¼ in).
3 At the top, connect the pipe to the gutter outlet using a swan-neck.
4 Measure the horizontal distance from the centre line of the outlet to

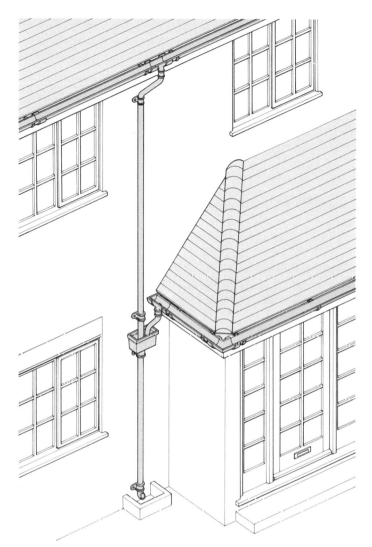

Left: Swan-necks are used to connect the outlet to the downpipe. Measure the distance and make them up on the ground rather than struggle at the top of a ladder. A hopper can be used instead of a 'Y' branch.

the centre of the downpipe. Chalk two parallel lines on the ground at the measured distance and lay two 112° offset bends down on those lines. Cut a length of pipe to fit.

Rainwater downpipe systems are designed for a loose, free fit. No solvent weld cement is needed, although it may occasionally be used to hold a shoe on the bottom of the pipe if a bracket cannot be fitted.

Joining to cast-iron

Although it is better to replace complete sections, an occasional join to cast-iron might be needed. Usually, plastic pipe will go into cast-iron pipe sockets easily. Reducing spigots are also available in some makes to

fit plain pipe or odd sizes.

If it helps lay the gutter out around the house on the ground to work out where the joints are to be placed. It might seem obvious to use complete lengths and fill in the gaps as you go but sometimes better use can be made of offcuts if you plan it properly first.

TO MAKE A PERFECT CUTTING LINE

Wrap a sheet of paper around the pipe and match the overlapping edges to form a perfect cutting guide. Cut the pipe with a fine-toothed saw.

EFFICIENT CENTRAL HEATING

Many central heating systems, while being perfectly well installed from a practical point of view, suffer from poor design. Badly placed radiators, which leave cold spots in the rooms, a mismatched boiler and controls and even the wrong size pipes on radiator circuits are all common faults. The fact that these problems exist in professional as well as DIY systems shows how complex central heating design has become.

The modern solution is to use the services of a specialist company who, with the aid of computer graphics, will produce a detailed drawing to work to. As yet, there is no computer capable of installing the system but, armed with such a drawing, it is possible for someone with a little experience of joining pipes and general DIY to tackle the job with confidence. As always, the more accurate you are at the planning stage, the better the results.

GOOD DESIGN

In order to provide a tailor-made system, rather than an off-the-shelf package, a designer will need to know details about your home.

To keep their fees low, designers usually work from a sketch and questionnaire completed by the client. These are some of the questions asked:

- Are the walls made of brick, breeze block or timber framed?
- Are they solid or cavity?
- Are the floors concrete or wood?
- Are the windows double-glazed?
- What size are the windows?
- What is each room used for, i.e. dining-room, bedroom?

If a bedroom is used as a study or a sitting-room, this will require a larger radiator than one normally used for just sleeping accommodation.

The sketch should also indicate:

- The preferred position of radiators, bearing in mind they are more efficient in the coldest part of the room, which is usually under the window.
- The position of the boiler, bearing in mind the restrictions based upon the siting of the flue.
- Which direction the house faces. The overall heat requirement is also influenced by whether the house is detached, whether it is at the top of a hill, even which part of the country it is in.

All heat requirements generally work on a minimum of 100mm- (4in-) thick loft insulation. If you cannot insulate above a room because of some restriction, this will have to be taken into account in calculating the size of the radiators.

Left: a well designed modern central heating system makes the whole house habitable in winter – there need be no cold spots or uninviting rooms.

The plan is drawn up, taking each floor separately. Pipe sizes are calculated to allow an adequate flow to the last radiator on the circuit, taking into account bend resistance.

The two circuits are connected by a vertical pipe run, which can be concealed in a cupboard. If the ground floor is solid, each group of radiators may be fed from the upper floor.

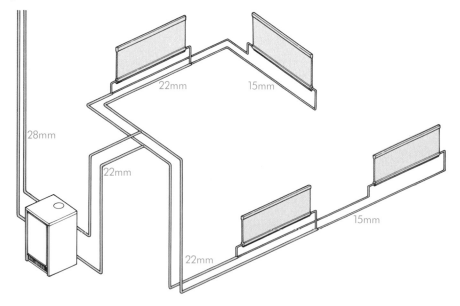

Above: Correct pipe sizes are essential for a good flow.

The typical central heating system

In a three-bedroom house, all the radiators are normally linked together so they can be controlled as one circuit.

Pipes are run beneath floorboards wherever possible but surface-run pipework is sometimes unavoidable.

Although in theory it is possible to run pipes under concrete floors by cutting channels in the screed this is rarely worth the great amount of upheaval for any more than a few feet. Instead the pipes are usually run down the walls from the circuit above. If this is done carefully it need not be

an eyesore. Pipe runs can often go inside cupboards or plastic trunking where they will not be noticed. One common trick is to run them up behind long curtains. When they are painted to match the decor, they will hardly be visible.

All dropped circuits must have draincocks at their lowest point. These can be attached to radiator tails for neatness or incorporated in elbows.

Generally, the radiators will be positioned against outside walls or beneath windows where they do the most good. Some professional installers, arguing that the heat is lost to

the outside, put radiators back to back in the middle of the house. This is really to save them pipe. The result is that cold spots are felt around the edge of the room and under the windows. If long curtains are to be used it is not worth having a radiator under the window. Often a small radiator on each side of the wall will do as much. Radiators are commonly single or double panel. To save wall space you can specify convector radiators which have a higher output per square metre. To fit under a bay window a radiator can be bent to the shape of a supplied template.

The order of work

This will be varied to suit individual circumstances.

1 Fix the radiator to the walls and run the pipes back to a central distribution point. All the returning radiator circuits must be joined together before they tee into the return pipe from the cylinder.

2 Install the indirect cylinder and connect it up to the cold water tank. It can then run from an electric immersion heater until the boiler is ready to take over the job of heating it. Connect and run the primary flow to the boiler position and connect the control valves.

3 Install the boiler in its position, wall-mounted or floor-standing, with the flue connected ready for testing and inspection.

4 The gas pipe can be left to a professional to install, or run in copper if this is included in the plan. The final connection to the gas pipe must be made and tested by a competent person.

5 The filling and top-up water for the heating system comes from the feed and expansion tank in the loft which can be installed with a stopcock on the supply to the ballvalve ready for filling.

A final check of all joints should be made before the system is flushed through and filled. Wire up all the control system, or call in an electrician. If after a couple of days all is well and no leaks are present, call a gas engineer to come and connect up.

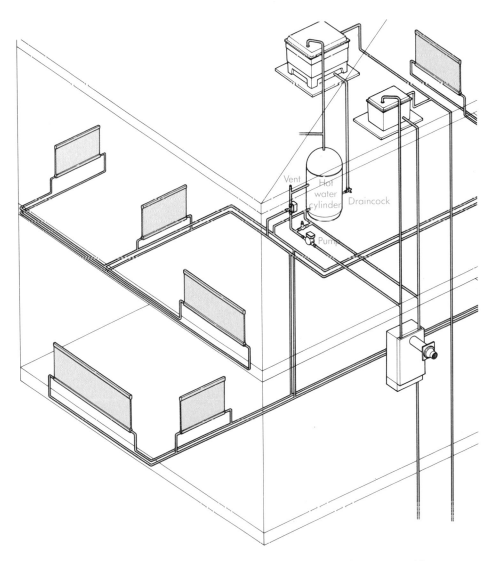

Above: a wall-mounted balanced flue boiler typically supplies pumped hot water to heat both the cylinder and central heating radiators via a diverter valve.

HEATING PROJECTS

Whether you are installing an entirely new system or updating an existing one, the projects covered in this section will help you to carry out the job in easy, manageable steps. With so many central heating products available, the designs and exact methods of fitting may vary from those shown here. Where there is a difference, manufacturers' fitting instructions must be followed in order to validate their guarantee.

Projects such as fitting thermostatic radiator valves or adding a radiator to an existing system will cause minimal interruption to the rest of the house. More ambitious jobs, like changing the boiler, should be tackled over two or three days. As with the plumbing projects, plan and prepare as much as possible in advance. Cutting off the existing system should be left until as late as possible to avoid inconvenience.

FITTING A RADIATOR

Even a so-called lightweight radiator is a heavy item. Most brick or block walls are firm enough to take the No. 12 roundhead screws but if not, use special fixings such as expanding bolts.

Plasterboard walls are never strong enough to carry such a weight. As it is unlikely that you will find two timbers exactly where the brackets have to go, an alternative surface must be provided. A sheet of 19-mm (¾-in) plywood slightly smaller than the radiator can be screwed to the timber structure and the brackets fixed with three or more screws in each. Alternatively, fix two 75mm × 25mm (3in × 1in) timber battens across the uprights and screw the brackets to those. The battens can be partly recessed into the plasterboard by cutting out strips of plasterboard with a craft knife.

Left: Radiators need a good circulation of air past them to distribute the heat. This radiator has been placed to heat both floors thereby eliminating the need for an upstairs landing radiator.

The radiator is usually positioned 150mm (6in) from the floor to allow air to convect freely. Similarly, air must flow out at the top. Adjust the brackets to dead level on their slots before fixing through the holes.

Try to position the radiators so that the pipes up to the valves avoid hitting joists. If you cannot avoid them, set the pipes in towards the middle of the radiator, just enough to clear the joist.

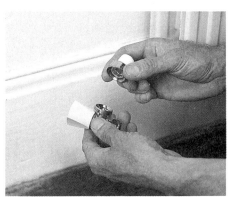

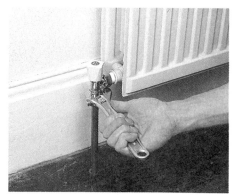

1 Detach the sensor head of a TRV. Undo the union nut to detach the threaded connector and wrap the thread with four or more turns of PTFE tape if not pre-coated.

2 Screw the connectors into the bottom tappings on the radiator. You may need an allen key for some valves; others take an open-ended adjustable spanner on the two flats.

3 Attach the body and insert the tail pipe into the bottom of the valve, making sure it falls upright into the hole drilled in the floorboards and is not binding on the board.

THERMOSTATIC RADIATOR VALVES

How they work

Thermostatic radiator valves sense the air temperature around a radiator and turn it off when that temperature reaches a pre-set level.

The valve has a body with a spring-return centre pin which closes off the flow, and a sensor head which is filled with gas or liquid. This expands as the temperature rises and pushes a plunger out to press on the spring-return spindle.

A thermostatic valve has one flow direction, which is marked on the body with an arrow. If the valve is only mountable in the upright position it must be on the flow pipe, so first find which is the flow pipe.

On existing systems

Switch on the heating from cold and feel both pipes on the radiator: the one which warms up first is the flow. Mark it so you will not forget.

Turn the water off or tie up the ballvalve to stop the feed and expansion tank filling. Turn off the controls and fuel supply. Drain through the draincock at a low point.

Instead of draining down the system, you can leave it to cool and then use a pipe-freezing kit to stem the flow in the pipe leading to the valve. You will also need to turn off the valve on the other side of the radiator. Be sure you have all the parts and tools close by.

On a new system

You will have to trace back along the pipework to the flow.

It may be necessary to extend the pipe slightly to fit the new valve. This is best done by cutting the pipe

Left: *Highly sensitive thermostatic radiator valves such as this one automatically control heat and help save on fuel bills. TRVs are fitted in place of the ordinary manual control valve usually on the flow pipe to the radiator.*

back and fitting a new section with a capillary joint. Do not forget to protect the skirting board with a heat resistant mat.

Fitting the new valve

The valve is fitted in the same way as a manual valve, except that the sensor head must not be attached until the fitting is complete.

Draining a radiator To remove a radiator for decorating behind or renewing (using the old valves), turn off the valves at each end. Place a large tray or square dish under one of the valves and gently undo the union nut, making sure the valve does not twist at the same time. The water from the radiator will drain into the dish. Bail out the excess into a bucket.

BE PREPARED

Keep the manual shut-off cap with your wallpapering equipment if you ever need to take the radiator off the wall for decorating.

The thermostatic control should not be relied upon to keep the flow shut off when the radiator is removed.

REMOVING THE OLD VALVE

Do this by undoing the nuts and unscrewing the tail from the radiator. You will probably need a special key to turn it, or a piece of flat metal, such as an old chisel blade. If the old compression ring is stuck on the pipe, gently cut through it—not the pipe.

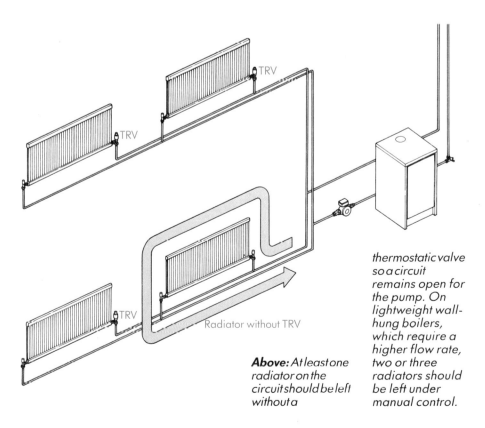

TRV

TRV

TRV

Radiator without TRV

Above: *At least one radiator on the circuit should be left without a*

thermostatic valve so a circuit remains open for the pump. On lightweight wall-hung boilers, which require a higher flow rate, two or three radiators should be left under manual control.

BOILERS

Boilers are now smaller, neater and more efficient than they were even a few years ago. If you have a boiler that is over 10 years old the chances are that it is costing you money in wasted fuel, and may also be taking up badly needed space. Wall-hung models with high outputs are available, but not all models are capable of serving gravity hot water circuits, so some alteration to the system might be needed.

Two important factors governing your choice of a boiler are the flue and the fuel. The following pages explain the difference between the different flues and give fitting details. Fan-assisted balanced flues are the most efficient and versatile in terms of fitting, and also look neater from the outside. The choice of fuel is largely a matter of what is available locally, as comparative running costs are likely to change.

Floor-standing boilers

Floor-standing boilers are still made in a range of both conventional and balanced flue models, so there is no need to abandon a useful floor space.

Floor-standing models are also predominantly fitted with cast-iron heat exchangers which are nearly all suitable for gravity hot water circuits, but this is a less efficient method of heating hot water than the fully-pumped method and ought to be abandoned if possible.

Some floor-standing models are now designed to fit under a standard 900mm (3 ft) worktop height. A slim-line version saves space but some clearance is necessary on all models for servicing, so do not take the actual dimensions as the maximum space. If there is a void behind the kitchen units this can be useful for running pipework, but can be difficult with the units in place.

Wall-hung boilers

These come with either cast-iron, aluminium or copper tube heat exchangers. The last two are for use with fully-pumped systems only. The low water content of the copper tube type can sound like a kettle boiling unless a flow of water is able to take the heat away. Pipe sizes might have to be increased to 28-mm along part of one radiator circuit and the pump 'head' increased to cope with this.

Another advantage of a fully-pumped system is that pipe connections can be kept to a minimum. One flow, one return and a gas supply are all that are needed. If the pipework is run straight up from the boiler it can be totally concealed in boxing. If the boiler forms part of a row of wall units, the top cupboards can be used to hide all the pipe runs and, perhaps, save notching above.

Combination boilers

'Combi' boilers provide heating and hot water with no need for a cylinder, a feed and expansion tank or a cold water tank. The space-saving advantage of having all this contained within one neat wall-hung unit is the main reason for the boilers' popularity in flats and small houses.

The biggest drawback is the slow flow of hot water, which makes it difficult to run a bath and another hot tap at the same time. In a flat with a limited number of people using the plumbing, this is a small inconvenience when weighed against having instant hot water on tap whenever it is needed.

Another peculiarity of this type of boiler is the fact that the radiators will go cold while the bath is being filled, but will automatically come back on when the tap is turned off.

Left and above: Wall-hung, floor-standing and wall-hung combination boilers look at home in any kitchen and match in well with units. If a boiler is completely hidden away it will need ventilation.

FUEL AND FLUES

With the exception of electricity, all other types of fuel give off hazardous fumes when burnt. The purpose of the flue is to dispose of those gases to the outside atmosphere.

Two methods of getting rid of the fumes (products of combustion) are used. One is the conventional flue, the other is the balanced flue.

The conventional flue This method of passing draught through the appliance and up the chimney requires a continuous fresh supply of oxygen coming into the room where the boiler is located. This must be provided by a permanent air brick or bricks to the outside. If the appliance is starved of oxygen the flue will not draw and fumes will come back out of the appliance. The first signs that this is happening are likely to be drowsiness and, possibly, sore eyes and sickness; death can follow quickly. For this reason, **a conventional flue must *never* be used in a bedroom.**

Existing chimneys must be lined, usually with a flexible stainless

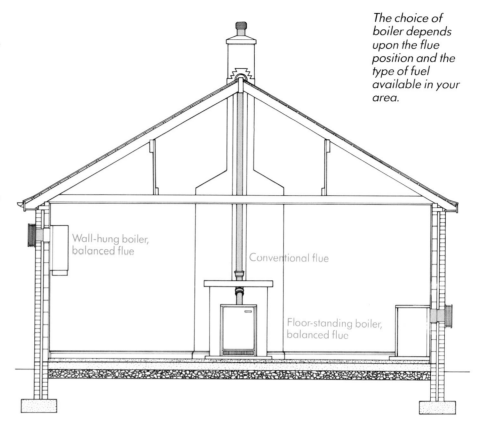

The choice of boiler depends upon the flue position and the type of fuel available in your area.

Wall-hung boiler, balanced flue

Conventional flue

Floor-standing boiler, balanced flue

steel liner to prevent acids attacking and damaging the brickwork and fumes leaking through defective joints or cracks.

Below: A balanced flue boiler.

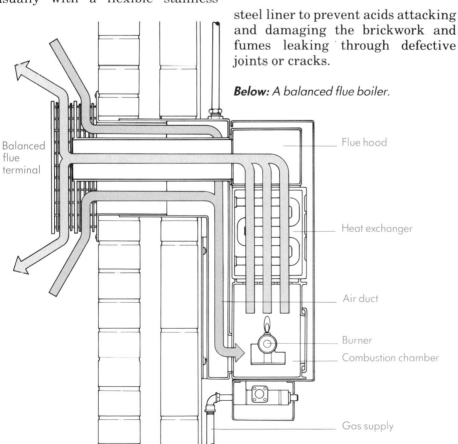

Balanced flue terminal

Flue hood

Heat exchanger

Air duct

Burner

Combustion chamber

Gas supply

The balanced flue This brings in air, drawn by the burning of the oxygen within the boiler and, at the same time, expels fumes to the atmosphere. This is done through a twin-walled ducting bringing air in through the outside and the hot gases out through the middle.

This type of boiler is often referred to as room-sealed, because the atmosphere in the room is not involved in any part of the operation. The balanced flue is therefore a safer method, provided the seals around the boiler casing are intact and the terminal outside is properly positioned. Problems can occur if the flue is too near an open window or air brick, as fumes can be drawn back into the room.

A fan-assisted balanced flue This works in the same way but because air is forced through the appliance, the flue duct and terminal are reduced in diameter and can be positioned closer to obstructions (see page 78). The airways through the boiler are also closer together and more efficient in extracting heat.

FITTING A BALANCED FLUE TERMINAL

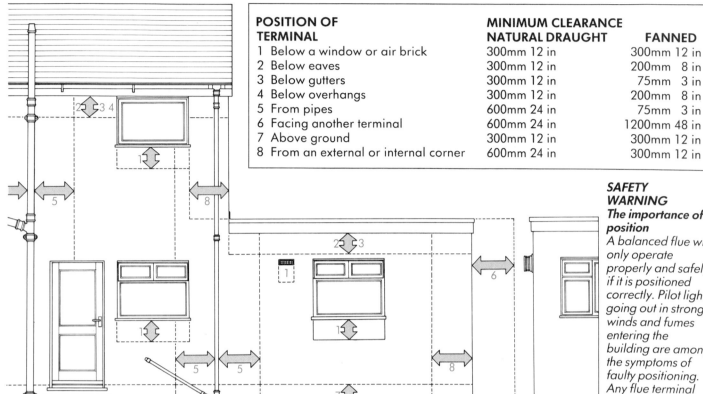

POSITION OF TERMINAL	MINIMUM CLEARANCE NATURAL DRAUGHT	FANNED
1 Below a window or air brick	300mm 12 in	300mm 12 in
2 Below eaves	300mm 12 in	200mm 8 in
3 Below gutters	300mm 12 in	75mm 3 in
4 Below overhangs	300mm 12 in	200mm 8 in
5 From pipes	600mm 24 in	75mm 3 in
6 Facing another terminal	600mm 24 in	1200mm 48 in
7 Above ground	300mm 12 in	300mm 12 in
8 From an external or internal corner	600mm 24 in	300mm 12 in

SAFETY WARNING
The importance of position
A balanced flue will only operate properly and safely if it is positioned correctly. Pilot lights going out in strong winds and fumes entering the building are among the symptoms of faulty positioning. Any flue terminal that can be touched should have a safety guard.

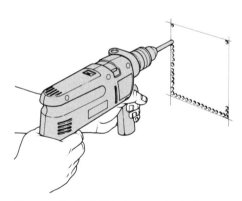

Above: *Chain drill holes to cut a hole.*

Above: *Cut out the middle with a bolster.*

Cutting for a box duct

Using the template or measurements supplied with the boiler, mark the outline of the hole on the inside wall, making sure it is level. Drill through the corners of the hole and redraw the shape on the outside wall. If you prefer, you can continue drilling all the way around the hole before cutting it out with a cold chisel, or you can simply start cutting away with the chisel.

Cutting for a fan-assisted duct

Hire a core cutter and a rotary hammer for a neater job. Always drill a pilot hole first and check on the outside for obstructions before cutting the larger hole. Many fan ducts are capable of being extended and turned to go through a wall other than the one on which the boiler is mounted. Transfer the measurements across with care if doing this.

Cutting by hand

Always nibble away at small pieces, rather than trying to remove big chunks in one go.

1 On cavity walls, take care not to drop any bricks between the walls.
2 Measure the thickness of the wall and adjust the terminal to suit, remembering to add the specified amount for joining into the boiler.
3 Wrap the duct joint with heat-resistant tape.
4 Insert the flue terminal and make any adjustment to line it up with the internal boiler hanging brackets.
5 Check the boiler brackets or studs are level.
6 Make good any damage to the internal plasterwork with sand and cement or plaster.
7 When cementing around the outside of the terminal wrap it in masking tape and newspaper to prevent lumps clogging the holes.
8 Hang the boiler on the flue plate with the sealing gasket in place.

FITTING A CONVENTIONAL FLUE

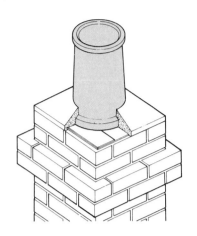

Above: Remove the old chimney pot, and make good the top. Thread in the liner leaving about 175mm (7 in) protruding.

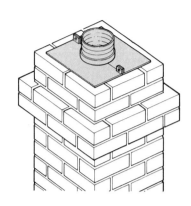

Above: Pour vermiculite insulation in around the liner. Fit the clamp plate with the bolt provided.

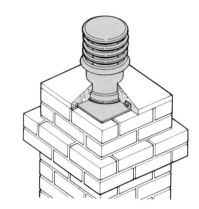

Above: Fit the terminal over the liner, then flaunch up the plate with three parts sharp sand and one of cement.

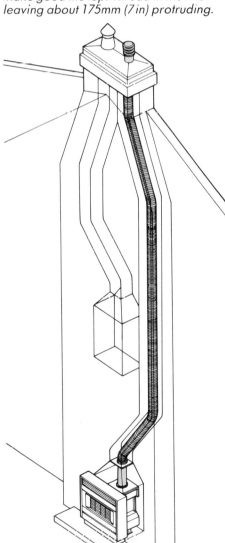

Above: A gas-fired back boiler with a conventional flue.

A conventional flue boiler can use an existing chimney with a liner or a prefabricated sectional chimney that slots together. Make sure the liner or chimney system is suitable for your boiler. Lining an existing chimney is a messy business. Clear the room or cover everything with dust sheets.

1 Remove the old fireplace to reveal the brick opening.
2 Sweep the chimney thoroughly.
3 Tape the sharp ends of the liner.
4 Drop a rope down the chimney and tie the flue liner to the end ready for a helper to gently pull it down.
5 Feed the liner down the chimney until gravity takes over. If it sticks on a chimney bend, pull it up slightly, rotate it and let it back down.
6 Make a plate out of a sheet of fire proof material such as calcium silicate board or aluminium to seal off the bottom of the chimney around the liner.

SAFETY WARNING
Hire a proper quick-assembly scaffold specially designed to give a working platform around a chimney. If you are not confident about carrying out this part of the job, call in a flue lining specialist.

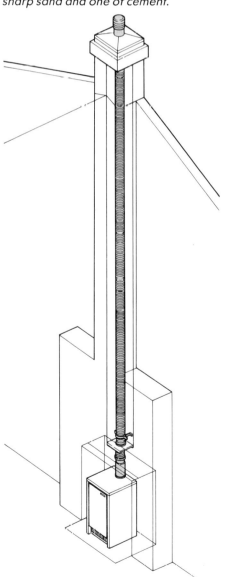

Above: A free-standing boiler with a conventional flue.

CONNECTING PIPES

Floor-standing boiler connections

The pipe runs to the cylinder must be in a minimum of 28-mm to help circulation. Any horizontal work should have at least twice as much vertical (head) from the base of the cylinder to the top of the boiler. If not, the circuit must be pumped.

It is essential that the vent pipe should rise continuously to discharge over the feed and expansion tank. Often the vent forms the gravity flow to the cylinder but if this is not convenient for the system a separate vent pipe can be used.

Use the template provided to determine the position of the flue terminal. Cut the hole in the wall and fix the flue first.

Remove the boiler casing and position the boiler temporarily. Work out the direction of the pipework, remembering that all the pipes will have to enter at the rear through the gap in the casing. The pipes must be run tight against the boiler sides, in order to leave room for the casing. It is a good idea to mark the intended positions of pipe runs on the wall. Fix pipe clips to the wall and make the main runs, so that only the final connections need to be made.

Withdraw the boiler so the fittings can be screwed in more easily.
- Wrap the 1-in male threads with PTFE tape and screw them into

the boiler so the elbows end up facing the right way round.
- Place a draincock in one of the bottom tappings.
- Use long radius bends, rather than sharp elbows, to keep the resistance in the system as a whole to a minimum.
- Plug any spare tappings with 1-in male iron plugs, which are usually provided with the boiler.
- Connect short runs of pipework to the boiler if this avoids struggling with awkward connections.
- Fit a safety valve on the gravity flow or return pipe, or into a spare tapping in the top of the boiler.

Fitting the casing Assemble the casing around the boiler using the screws provided. Some models have an earthing wire to connect between the body of the boiler and the exposed metalwork of the casing. If your boiler does not have this a paint-cutting star washer is provided to make a good earthing connection to a bracket.

Pump positioning Make sure the pump is mounted according to manufacturer's instructions and that it leaves room for the casing to fit properly. If there is not enough room mount the pump on wall brackets outside the boiler.

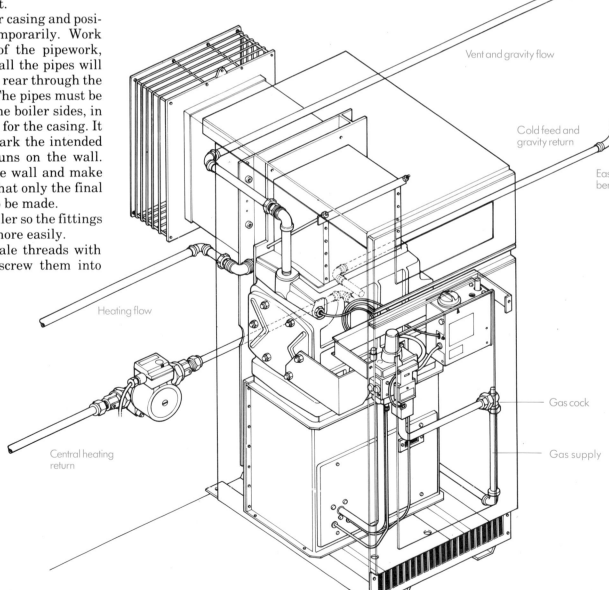

Vent and gravity flow

Cold feed and gravity return

Easy bend

Heating flow

Central heating return

Gas cock

Gas supply

Right: A floor-standing boiler with a cast-iron heat exchanger, using a gravity hot water-pumped heating system with each circuit coming in and out on opposite sides. All connections (except the gas) are screwed in using PTFE tape.

WALL-HUNG BOILER

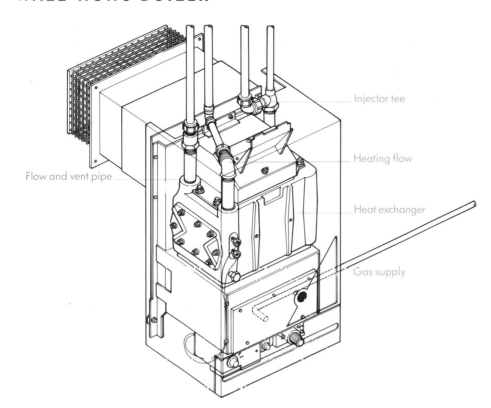

Injector tee

Heating flow

Heat exchanger

Flow and vent pipe

Gas supply

Kettling This is a term used to describe the boiling noise often heard in low water content wall-hung boilers. The sound is usually the result of too slow a flow rate through the boiler or too much gas. Try turning the pump speed up to maximum. If this creates too much of a whirring noise it is likely that the pipe sizes on the main radiator circuit will have to be increased to 28 mm for most of their length to cope with this rate of heat. Another alternative is to have the gas input rate turned down. Provided this still provides sufficient heat it can be left like that. A sign that the boiler is not powerful enough is white steam constantly coming out of the flue terminal.

Left: An easy conversion from floor-standing to wall-hung boilers can be made by changing to a fully pumped system. Only three pipes need then be connected to the boiler.

Joining to pipes

A copper heat exchanger This type of wall-hung boiler has two 28-mm copper tubes with plain ends coming out of the top. These are ready for fitting with compression joints to the flow and return pipes, which also serve as the feed and vent pipe for some of their length.

Cast-iron wall-hung boiler The threaded tappings are identical to its floor-standing counterpart and, provided it is suitable for gravity circulation, can be connected in the same way.

If a fully-pumped system is used with a cast-iron boiler, connect to one of the top tappings and one of the bottom tappings. The remaining ones can be either blocked off, or used for the safety valve and a separate cold feed and vent pipe.

The fittings should be screwed into the back of the boiler before it is hung. If at all practicable, join short lengths of pipework to the fittings to bring the connections above the top of the boiler. Tape the pipe ends temporarily to stop debris falling into the heat exchanger.

Adapting a gravity system

An existing gravity flow and return can often be twinned to the heating side of a fully-pumped system and brought in and out of the boiler as a single circuit on 28-mm pipes. The feed and vent pipe must be reconnected to the pipework within 150mm (6 in) of each other in order to prevent water being forced over or sucked in the vent pipe by the action of the pump. The connections should not be made on bends. A good method is to use a purpose-made air separator. The old feed and vent connections at the cylinder can be cut short and left as standpipes with air cocks on the pipes. The circuits are then controlled by two electric zone valves linked to thermostats.

In order to keep water moving through the heat exchanger to clear residual heat for a few minutes after the valves are closed, a by-pass circuit must be incorporated after the pump and at least 1m (3 ft) away from the boiler. The switching of the pump overrun is controlled automatically by a circuit within the boiler.

Above: A modern wall-hung boiler has simple connections to provide separate heating and hot water and it is ideal where space is scarce.

COMBINATION BOILERS

How they work

Mains pressure water comes into the boiler and is heated by passing through a mini cylinder. The flow of water from the mains switches on the burner, the pump and a diverter valve, which sends water from the heat exchanger around the cylinder and back again. When central heating is required, the electronic programmer switches on the burner and the pump and diverts the flow to the heating circuit. The expansion in the heating system as the water gets hotter is taken up by a pressure vessel inside the boiler casing. This extra pressure is higher than that of an open vented system and requires good quality radiator valves to prevent small leaks.

Although combination boilers are

methodically, finishing each connection before starting the next.

The mains water The boiler should have a strainer fitted into the pipework at some point to keep small

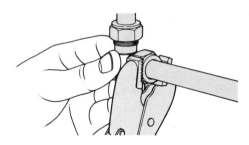

Connections are made with a spanner or wrench using compression fittings.

Built in controls simplify wiring and give options of heating and hot water.

by far the most complicated of all boilers in terms of what lies within their casing, from an installation point of view they could not be more straightforward.

The confusing maze of pipework inside the boiler eventually comes out of the bottom all clearly marked and ready for connecting to the system with compression fittings.

Fitting

If all the pipes to the boiler are run in the right order, so there is no need for any last-minute ducking and diving, the finished job will be neat.

Once the boiler has been hung on the wall with the flue in place, screw a row of pipe brackets into the wall exactly below the connections, so all pipes come up parallel.

The pipes can be run in any order but it is often best to work through

particles out of the gas/water valve.

A 15-mm isolating service valve is usually incorporated in the connector. If it is not, fit one immediately before connecting to the boiler.

The hot connection The pipe out to the taps can be run in 15-mm pipework, since it is under mains pressure, though the flow rate is slowed down. A valve is not needed on the hot supply – it is controlled by the cold water going into the boiler.

Central heating The flow and return for central heating could be run in 22-mm or 28-mm, depending on the size and make of the boiler. A ballofix service valve can be fitted to each pipe to provide a means of isolating the heating circuit, so long as the boiler has an internal by-pass.

Filling up

The central heating circuit is filled

through a hosepipe with a permanently connected double-check valve assembly. This is connected temporarily from the rising main to a valve on the heating circuit.

Above: A water conditioner prevents scale from building up in the boiler heat exchanger and also inhibits scale in the pipework and taps.

Above: Complicated combination boilers are surprisingly simple to install, so long as you do not get your pipes crossed. The gas connection should be left to a qualified professional.

INSTALLING HEATING AND HOT WATER CONTROLS

In this computerized age, modern central heating controls have become very sophisticated. Or have they? Companies may offer to update your existing controls with 'electronic energy management systems' that claim to save up to 40 per cent of your fuel bills. Depending on the cost of installation it may take several years to recover your costs, by which time you may need a new heating system anyway.

If a heating system is running at 40 per cent below efficiency because of inadequate controls, even if only during the summer, there is almost certainly something that can be done on a DIY basis to improve it dramatically; the pay-back period is likely to be months rather than years. Before deciding what improvements can be made, you will need to know how up-to-date your controls are or, for a new system, what controls are needed.

The route to efficiency

The programmer Despite the flashing lights and digital readouts of the more 'hi-tech' central heating programmers, their essential function is to switch on and off. In many ways they are no more complicated than a pair of light switches on a timer.

The energy saving capability of this piece of equipment comes in its ability to turn the system off when you are asleep or away from home and not therefore in need of central heating.

Modern programmers have added days of the week to their menu so if you plan a Sunday-morning lie in, and tell the programmer, it will delay the switching-on time. There is also a programmer that will give the heating a head start over the hot water, or vice versa, so that a smaller boiler can be used.

Thermostats To make any significant savings, a system must have remote thermostats which sense the temperature of the hot water cylinder and the temperature of the radiators. The thermostat on the boiler should only be there as a back-up to stop the boiler overheating. Systems that use the boiler thermostat to control the hot water or radiator temperatures are working inefficiently.

Motorized valves The third part of a modern control system is the motorized valve or valves. This device is like an automatic stopcock which turns off the flow of water around a particular circuit.

The thermostats tell these valves to turn on/off or divert water from one circuit to the other.

Above: 7-day digital programmer, mechanical programmer with two on-off cycles per day, preset frost stat (top right) and room thermostat.

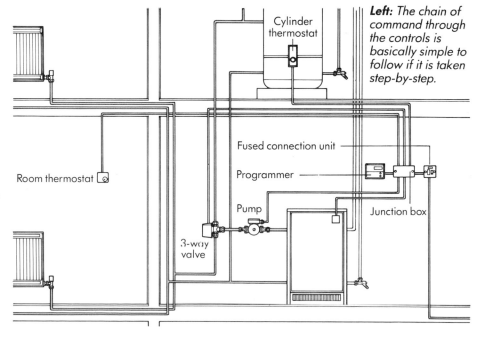

Left: The chain of command through the controls is basically simple to follow if it is taken step-by-step.

WIRING UP

Packaged systems

The easiest way to buy a control system is in a complete package. If you prefer to use individual components you will not have the benefit of colour-coded numbered connections.

1 Start by screwing the terminal box to the wall or floor near the motorized valves.

2 Fit the programmer to the wall in a place where it is easy to operate but also close to the boiler and controls.

3 Attach the cylinder thermostat to the cylinder, using the wire or band to hold it against the outside wall of the cylinder. If the cylinder is insulated with foam, cut out a rectangle with a craft knife to expose the copper. The thermostat should be in the bottom third of the cylinder, away from the cold feed entry point.

4 Screw the room thermostat 1.5m (5ft) high on the wall in the hall or living-room. It must be away from any heat source or draughts.

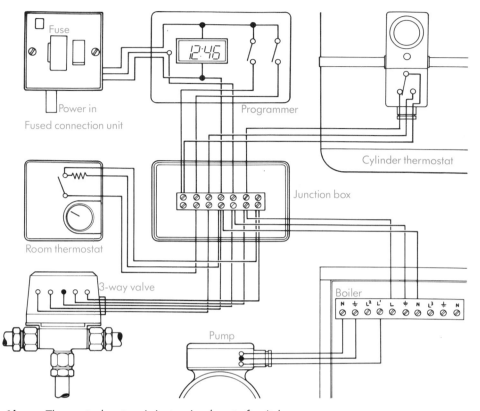

Above: *The control system is just a simple set of switches.*

An existing system

You will need to drain down the entire heating system before plumbing the motorized valves in to the pipework. Keep the arrows (stamped on the side) in the direction of the flow. Make sure the vent pipe to the boiler is not obstructed by the fitting of the valve and that there is still a route for the cold feed to the boiler. A diverter or flowshare three-port valve must form a tee with the flow from the boiler coming in, being divided out to the radiator and hot water circuits. If this is not possible, because of the pipework layout, use two separate zone valves, which can be placed virtually anywhere on the circuits after the vent pipe.

Two-port zone valves can also be used to cut off circuits not needed during the day. This could be done with a time switch so that the bedrooms receive heat only during the morning and evening.

Fill the system to check the plumbing connections before beginning the wiring.

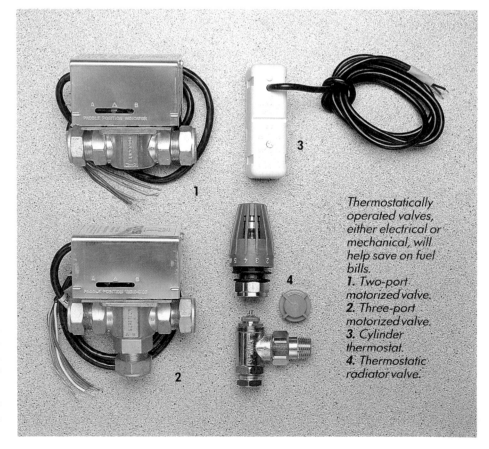

Thermostatically operated valves, either electrical or mechanical, will help save on fuel bills.
1. Two-port motorized valve.
2. Three-port motorized valve.
3. Cylinder thermostat.
4. Thermostatic radiator valve.

WIRING TO THE MAINS SUPPLY

Running cables

Cables enter components through special entry points, except for motorized valves which have short flexes to connect inside a junction box. All joins must be made within junction boxes. The cables can be buried in walls inside plastic conduit, or run in mini-trunking on the surface.

- Clip cables in cupboards and lofts.
- Drill small holes 75mm (3 in) down for running the cables through floor joists clear of nails.
- Avoid cables touching hot pipes, and use heat-resistant cable in the boiler casing.

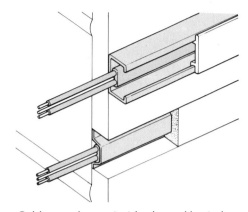

Cables can be run inside channel buried beneath the plaster or surface-mounted in mini-trunking. Buried cables must always run horizontally or vertically.

SAFETY WARNING

When wiring up a new circuit it is always safer to start from the end and work backwards towards the mains connection. If you are working on an existing circuit, be certain to turn off at the fusebox and remove the fuse or circuit-breaker.

Making connections

1 Remove a section of the outer casing and bare the ends of cables 3mm (⅛ in) ready for connection.
2 Cover earth wires with green and yellow plastic sleeving.
3 Wrap a small red flag of tape around any black wires which are being used for lives.
4 Follow the wiring diagram here, or the one supplied with your controls if they are different.

How it works

Current comes from the mains to the programmer where it powers the time-clock and carries on through the switches to the thermostats. If the room or hot water cylinder is cold, the thermostats will 'call' for heat and the current will be passed into the junction box to connect with the appropriate motorized valve(s). These, when open, activate a micro-switch within their casing.

This passes current back along the

flex to the junction box to connect with the boiler power supply. The live current switches on the boiler and, depending on the make, starts the pump directly from the terminal box or through the boiler. Going through the boiler allows the pump overrun (fitted on some boilers) to operate after the boiler is switched off.

Thermostats have a switching interval of about 2°C (4°F) between the make and break positions.

Connecting to the mains

The main power to a central heating system can be spurred off the ring main or run from a spare fuseway. If you do not feel confident about this part of the job, call in a professional.

- The supply can come from the back of a 13-amp ring main socket or other permissible connection point to a switched fused connection unit (FCU) with a neon light (to show when the system is on).
- The cable to the FCU must be 2.5mm² twin and earth. From the FCU to the programmer the supply is run in 1.5mm² twin and earth cable or 0.75mm² three-core flex. Ensure that the outer insulation of flex is firmly held in the cord grips.
- Fit a 3-amp fuse to the switch only when all the covers have been replaced and no live wires are exposed.
- Do not run the system, even for a few seconds, without water.
- For the testing of electrical connections the gas need not be connected, but some boilers will show a fault and cut out if no gas comes through.

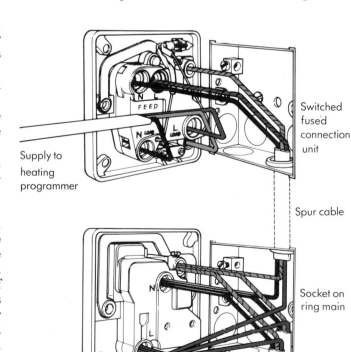

Supply to heating programmer

Switched fused connection unit

Spur cable

Socket on ring main

Left: A switched fused connection unit with a removable fuse and a neon light indicating ON is the safest way to connect to the mains.

CONTROLLING A GRAVITY SYSTEM

Feed and
expansion tank

Rising main

*Wiring up a gravity
circuit to give
greater control is a
cost effective job.
This system was a
suitable case for
treatment: a gravity
hot water circuit
with only the boiler
thermostat
controlling the
temperature.*

Vent pipe to
cold water
storage

Hot supply
to bathroom
and kitchen

Cylinder
thermostat

Cold supply
to cylinder

Room thermostat

Programmer

To radiators

Boiler

Pump

From
radiators

Saving your money

Of the many money-saving improvements that can be made to an inefficient control system, adding a cylinder thermostat is the single most cost-effective. It is even more appealing when you discover that the components are inexpensive and the plumbing work nil. To save more, it is possible to add a motorized valve or two to give greater control in the winter as well.

The cause of the problem

Before the cylinder thermostat was added to the system, the boiler switched on and off to satisfy its own thermostat. This meant that during the non-heating season, when the programmer was set to 'hot water only', the boiler would keep switching on and off for the entire period. The cylinder, which may well have been hot within the first 45 minutes, had no further need of the boiler, but the boiler thermostat would keep the boiler hot anyway. All the heat was wasted, mostly up the flue, and every time it escaped the boiler would switch back on to top it up again. During the times when the central heating was running, the boiler would have more to do and the efficiency would improve.

The cure

1 Strap a cylinder thermostat to the cylinder wall somewhere on the lower third of the cylinder.
2 Run a three-core-and-earth cable (such as those used for two-way switching) between the cylinder and a junction box.
3 Screw a junction box beside the heating programmer or, if it is a large one, you may be able to use it to make the connections.
4 Bare the ends of the cable 3mm (1/8 in) and connect them into the cylinder thermostat as follows:
Red to common.
Blue to the terminal that breaks on 'calling' for heat.
Yellow to the terminal that makes on 'calling' for heat.
Earth to earth.
Turn off the electricity supply to the system and remove the fuse.
5 Remove the cover of the programmer and remove the wire from the 'Hot Water On' terminal.
6 Connect this to the red wire from the cylinder thermostat.
7 Connect the yellow wire to the 'Hot Water On' terminal just vacated.
8 Connect the blue wire to the live supply on the pump after it has been through the room thermostat.

Now the boiler will only start up when either the cylinder thermostat or the room thermostat 'calls' for heat. Even though the programmer is switched on, the system still will not work so long as the temperature requirements are satisfied.

This controls the cylinder temperature in the summer but in the winter, when the radiators are being heated, the cylinder temperature will have to be the same, which is usually far too hot for the tap water and too cold for the radiators.

The answer to this problem is to fit a two-port 28-mm motorized valve on the cylinder return pipe – not the flow because that is also the vent pipe. The wiring is the same as that for a fully-pumped system, except that the auxiliary switch from the valve goes to the boiler only.

PUMP FITTING AND CHANGING

Some central heating pumps only last for two or three years, while others go on for ever. This can be more to do with the system they are in than the pump itself. There are a limited number of things that can be tried to revive a pump but if none of these work a new one must be fitted. Fortunately, they are designed for quick and easy changeover.

Removing a faulty pump

The first step is to turn off the system and let things cool down. A jammed pump will often be too hot to touch. Note down the direction of flow signified by an arrow on the pump.

If there are pump valves on either side, turn them off. Some have a slot which you turn through 90° to close. If there are no valves, drain the system. Turn off the water going into the feed and expansion tank. Attach a hosepipe to a draincock lower than the pump and run it outside. Then open up the draincock.

Undo the union nuts, anticlockwise, on each side of the pump with a large pair of grips or pump pliers. If they are stuck, spray them with penetrating oil and come back in half an hour. If they are still stuck, undo the air bleed screw on the pump to drain the body and use a hair drier on the nuts. This might soften any jointing compound inside them.

Freeing a jammed pump

Do not always assume a pump is jammed. Listen to it through a screwdriver handle – if you cannot hear a humming there may be a loose connection.

If a pump is jammed it can sometimes be started by:
- Turning up the speed regulator.
- Turning the manual restart slot, in the middle behind the chrome cap, with a screwdriver (you can sometimes feel it binding: it should be free and smooth).
- Gently tapping the body with a hammer to loosen any rust holding the impeller.

If none of these methods work, turn off the unions and remove the pump. Wash it through and turn by poking a screwdriver into one end. If it will not run freely, fit a new one.

Pump life can be considerably increased if the system is descaled and then treated with a corrosion inhibitor.

Fitting a new pump

If the gap between the unions is larger than the new pump, screw on a special adaptor with a washer in between.

Lightly smear silicone grease around the threads of the new pump to assist future removal. Clean off the flanges of the old unions with a

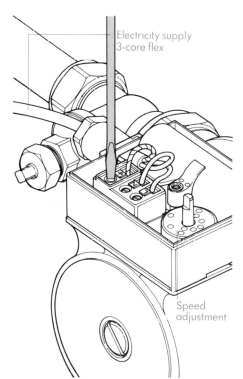

Above: Easy connections to the pump are made through clearly marked terminals.

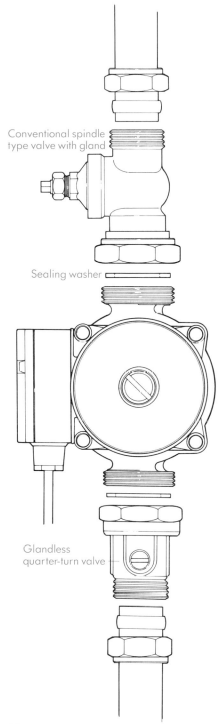

Above: A pump must have isolating valves on either side to allow removal.

piece of emery cloth.

Fit the new washers supplied to the unions.

With the arrow pointing the right way, insert the pump and hand-tighten the unions. Use the wrench to give a final turn but do not overtighten – you never know when you will want to take it off. Turn on the water and bleed the air through the screw.

GETTING THE SYSTEM GOING

With all the plumbing and electrics complete, the system is almost ready to go. It should be filled with water and tested for leaks before it is run, then thoroughly flushed through after temporarily removing the pump and bridging with pipe. The gas connection should also be made at this stage so that the boiler is ready for its first hot run, after which it can be drained down to help remove fluxes not cleared by the cold water.

An old system that has been altered, perhaps by fitting a new boiler, must be cleaned with chemical additives. All systems will give improved life and efficiency if they are treated with corrosion and scale inhibitor during their final topping up, but this should be delayed until you are sure there are no leaks which require draining down again. Finally, the radiators should be balanced to even out the heat so that they all run at the same temperature.

GAS CONNECTIONS

The final gas connection is a job that must be left to an expert. If there is gas already in the room, serving a cooker or an old boiler, it can be used to supply the boiler provided that the pipe has a large enough diameter. If it is too small, a new gas pipe might have to be run from the meter. It is now common practice to run gas pipes in copper outside the building and to bring the branches to the appliances in through sleeved holes. This method has safety advantages, but is primarily done to make life easier for the gas fitter and cheaper for the customer.

Running gas pipes

Inside a building, gas pipe is subject to more stringent rules than water pipes. Some gas fitting companies still use threaded iron pipe which is strong, but prone to rust. Others have changed to copper, which is a lot easier to fit. The disadvantage of copper is its susceptibility to damage. When it is used for water pipe, a nail through the middle usually results in no more than a bit of mess; a nail through a gas pipe might not even be detected until a quantity of gas has built up beneath the floor.

Gas fitters have to be aware of this when running pipes and should try to keep them out of harm's way. One simple method is to mark the top of the boards with a pen to show the line of the gas pipe underneath. Pipes buried in walls cannot be marked but damage is more likely to be noticed by the smell of the gas.

A gas engineer puts the whole system, new and old, on test with a

There is a legal requirement that only competent persons shall work on gas appliances and supply pipes. This part of the job must be carried out by a professional with special equipment for adjusting the pressure to the burners and checking that the whole system is free from leaks.

manometer to check for any pressure loss over a set period. Any fault might just as easily be with the old pipework as the new run to the boiler. Small leaks beneath ground floors can go undetected for years.

The manometer is also used to check and adjust the burner pressure on the boiler which sometimes needs setting to suit the heating load. Adjustments might also be needed to stop whistling in the burners or resonance in the flue before the boiler is given a clean bill of health.

Servicing. A service contract is the best way to keep the gas boiler running efficiently and safely. A whole-system service and repair contract covers parts and labour and

is available on DIY and professionally installed systems provided they have been correctly installed.

Once you have been signed up on a whole-system service contract you will have the peace of mind that an emergency call-out service offers and no further expenses even in the events of parts failure.

The gas service engineer will advise on any necessary alterations needed to meet their strict standards. They will also check the positions and sizes of fresh-air ventilators to the room or cupboard in which the boiler may be housed.

If any work is required not on the gas side of the appliance you may carry it out yourself or ask them to do it for you.

FILLING AND FLUSHING

Why flush?

Solder, flux, copper swarf and iron filings are just some of the things that can cause a considerable amount of damage, even in a new system. It is not uncommon for radiators to develop pinhole leaks within a few months as a result of impurities, and for pumps to grind to a halt. The operation of valves can also be upset by debris which becomes lodged in their mechanisms. Flushing a system through to remove debris can be a tedious business, particularly when you are filling up for the fifth time in succession. However, to skimp on this part of the job is to undo much of the previous good work and also invites trouble later on when you should be enjoying the fruits of your labour.

How to flush

The initial flushing of a new or existing system must be done with the pump removed, in order to prevent any debris catching in the pump and also to make sure that the water flows quickly through the pipes.

Bridge the gap left by the removal of the pump using a plain length of copper pipe between the pipes.

Start with the draincock fully open and the radiators closed, then open up the radiator valves and vent the radiators through the air release points at the top. When the system is full, open the draincock and let the water flow at maximum. Repeat this process several times until the water is cleared and you are satisfied that every part of the system has been filled and drained at least twice.

In an old system, remove the radiators with the system drained and take them outside where you can wash them through with a hose until the water runs clear.

After the initial flushing, replace the pump and fill the system. Run the system cold (with gas off), then turn off and drain down.

Several chemical descalents and flushing additives are available to clean the system further. However,

if you have a new system and decide not to use them, turn off the system and drain it while hot just to remove the fluxes and grease held in the hot water.

Vents

Cylinder

Thermostat

Boiler

Pump

Feed and expansion tank

Left: The system should be flushed through to clean it out.

Scale problems

Scale can start building up in a system from the very first day. The rate varies with water hardness but even 1mm ($\frac{1}{32}$in) of scale coating in a boiler can waste 10 per cent of the fuel. In very hard water areas, that figure could grow to 30% after five years.

Apart from the waste, scale is often accompanied by banging and even quite alarming howling noises in the boiler. Fortunately, there is a cure which will give a badly scaled system a new lease of life and improve efficiency. In all but severe cases it involves a chemical treatment to remove the scale, followed by a neutralizing additive.

Old systems will need descaling if corrosion inhibitor is to be added (see page 90).

All chemicals are added through the feed and expansion tank. Drain off some of the water from the system first and turn off the supply to the ballvalve to stop it refilling until you require it.

Follow the instructions closely, especially those concerning health and safety.

The system must be run hot for the specified period – usually up to 24 hours – but in some cases a week on a normal cycle. If the system is old (over 12 years), the descalent might uncover leaks which have been sealed by scale. An inhibited descaler, with no bite, should be used instead, though the benefits will not be so great in terms of efficiency and a new boiler would be better.

DESCALING AND CORROSION PROOFING

Causes of corrosion in central heating systems

- Water can be corrosive to lead-soldered joints and other metals.
- Oxygen in the water which attacks radiators and cast-iron boilers.
- Electrolytic action, particularly between copper and zinc-coated steel or aluminium.
- Impurities in the water such as fluxes and iron filings.

Black or red water If the system has been running for more than a few weeks the colour of the central heating water is a good guide to the extent of corrosion in your system.

Black water Black magnetite as a result of electrolytic action can be cured by adding corrosion inhibitor.

Orange/red water Oxygen is being introduced into the system. This will require alterations to the pipework before adding corrosion inhibitor.

Selecting the corrosion inhibitor

There are a number of different types of corrosion inhibitor, made for different boilers. You will need to know if you have a cast-iron boiler or a copper tube type (see page 76) and whether you have steel or aluminium radiators.

Air problems

If air is getting into the system, the first place to look is in the feed and expansion tank. Sit beside it with a good light and examine it under all functions of the programmer. That is, water only, heating and water, and heating only, if you have it.

Check for air being sucked in through the vent pipe by placing a wet thumb lightly over the end.

Air may also be sucked in through the pump unions around the nuts, so check these with a wet finger.

If any water comes out of the vent pipe try turning the pump speed down one setting. If the system still operates properly, leave it set there. If it does not, the pump must be set higher and the pipework changed. The easiest way of overcoming these problems is to fit a purpose-made air

Above: Central heating components are stored in plain water on the right and corrosion inhibitor on the left.

Top right: Pipe blocked through scale build-up.

Right: Corrosion inhibitor is added to the water through the feed and expansion tank.

separator. This is a copper chamber joined in to the flow pipe from the boiler. It provides a chance for the water to slow down. As the water is beaten around the chamber it loses some of its oxygen up the remaining vent section. The cold feed is joined into the side to complete the ideal arrangement.

Another possible cause of air being drawn into some systems is when bleeding an upstairs radiator while the pump is running. Turn down the room thermostat to stop the pump, then bleed the radiator again so that the head of water in the feed and expansion tank forces out the air.

Right: Sludge build-up in radiators results in cold spots at the bottom. Remove the radiator and flush through with a hosepipe.

BALANCING THE SYSTEM

What balancing does

The term central heating suggests a boiler in the middle of the house spreading its heat out evenly to the surrounding radiators. In fact, this is rarely the case. More often, the radiators branch off from the main larger-bore pipework in a fairly haphazard way, diving this way and that to serve any nook and cranny that you have chosen to put a radiator in.

Water, even when pumped, will always find the route of least resistance; so some radiators will receive a lot of the flow and therefore the heat, while others receive next to nothing. This problem often develops when a radiator is removed for decorating or one is added to the system.

The solution is to balance the system so the easy routes are made harder and the hard ones easier. This is done by the lockshield valves on the radiators and if necessary a larger lockshield valve on the cylinder return pipe.

Lockshield valves The wheel valve on a radiator is for turning it on and off. The valve on the other side is the lockshield valve. In fact, they are often identical valves with different caps and can be interchanged, since

Right: Using a pair of clip-on pipe thermometers, balance radiator flow and return by turning the lockshield valve until a temperature difference of 11°C shows.

it is not necessary for either one to be on a particular side. Once a side has been chosen, it should be set and left so all day-to-day adjustments are made on the same valve.

How to do it Start with the system running at normal temperature with both the hot water and heating operating. Open (anticlockwise) both valves fully on each radiator.

Start from the first radiator on the circuit; this is usually the hottest. Turn down the lockshield valve until a temperature difference of 11°C (about 20°F) is reached. The easiest way to find this is with a pair of small clip-on pipe thermometers.

Work your way around the sys-

tem, following as near as you can the order of the radiators, and adjust each one to work at the same temperature drop. Use the thermometers to measure the overall flow and return.

Hot water balancing

As the pipework to the cylinder coil is usually shorter it provides an easier route for the water from the boiler. To overcome this some systems are designed with a Ballofix valve to choke off the circulation. This is usually placed immediately next to the cylinder on the return to the boiler. If the cylinder is taking more than half an hour to heat up from cold it is worth opening the valve slightly.

If the radiators are not getting as hot as they should particularly if the boiler is switching off on its internal thermostat then it is worth closing the valve to give the radiators a bigger share. Again the use of pipe thermometers takes out the guess work as you can see the effect of adjusting the valves. Remember that the cylinder and heating must be started from cold to give a true comparison, but do not spend hours trying to achieve specific figures because the demand will have diminished.

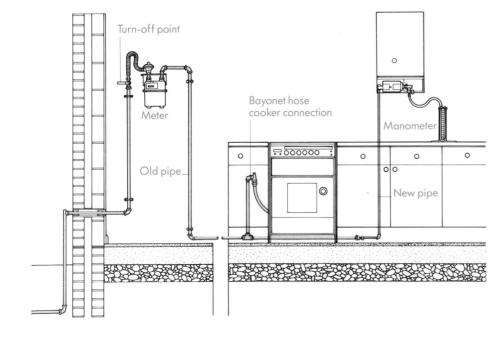

Left: A manometer is used to adjust the gas pressure and give a final check on the soundness of the pipework. The required boiler pressure should be obtainable with the gas cooker running.

THE FINISHING TOUCHES

After all the hard work has been done and the system is running as it should, with no leaks, creaks, or bumps in the night, it is easy to neglect the finishing touches. Such a simple job as insulating pipework might seem unimportant in the summer when it is difficult to imagine frosts, but a few months on, it can mean the difference between coming home to warmth and comfort, or to a flood.

Screwing down floorboards is another job that is often put off indefinitely, just in case there is a need to lift one up again to gain access to a joint. Apart from the annoying creaks from loose boards, there can be a tendency for boards to curl if they are left unfixed. Then, when you do eventually get around to screwing them down, they may even split down the middle as the screws pull them flat.

WHAT NEEDS INSULATING?

Any pipes outside the heated area of the building need insulating to protect them from the effects of frost and, in the case of heating pipes, to keep heat in. This includes:

- All pipes in the loft, even the overflows from the tanks.
- Pipes under wooden ground floors.
- Pipes outdoors, which must be wrapped in waterproof insulation.
- Heating pipes, where the heat serves no useful purpose, can also be insulated to conserve heat for the radiators.
- Tanks, hot water cylinders and even flue pipes passing through lofts should also be insulated.

Existing pipes

Following the experience of some very severe winters, the standards for pipe insulation have been dramatically improved. If you have the old hair-felt lagging or open-textured foam sleeving around your pipes it is worth upgrading it to the new thicknesses.

This can be done by adding more lagging over the top or removing the old and using new sleeving. In the case of some of the old, cheaper foam types, they may have disintegrated anyway.

It is important when insulating pipes to be thorough. A well insulated plumbing system can suffer from a burst pipe because of one single joint being left exposed.

Most preformed insulation sleeving comes semi-split. If it is being threaded on to pipes such as the vent pipe there is no need to split it completely, but almost everywhere else the split will need to be completed with a blunt knife.

Secure split lengths to the pipes with plastic pull ties or adhesive tape. Special glue is also available for joining the split.

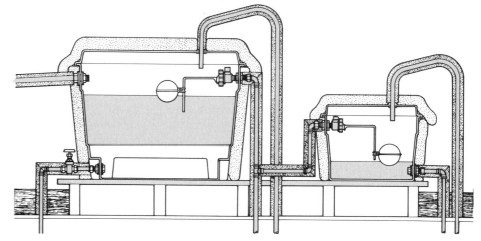

Above: Insulate over the top of tanks but leave the underside free to gain heat from the house.

Below: Mitre right angles and make release cuts on the inside of bends to ensure a good fit.

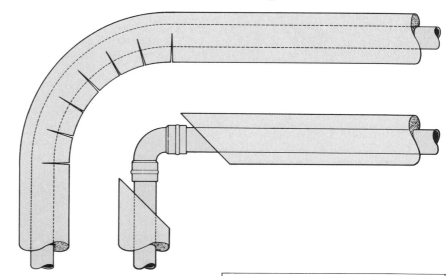

INSULATING LEAD AND IRON PIPES

Pipe insulation comes in metric sizes based on standard copper pipe sizes. For lead or iron pipes in imperial sizes, select the metric equivalent for the next size up.

REPLACING BOARDS

Old boards

If floorboards have been carefully removed in complete pieces there is every chance that they will go back in something like their original condition, but split or short boards that make a jigsaw puzzle of the floor are not worth keeping. Even if you can manage to work out where they go, it is difficult to refix them, bearing in mind you have a limited area in which to put screws if you are to miss the pipes underneath. Do not use nails, as they will work free from their holes after being refixed and the boards will crack.

New boards

New timber boards are certain to shrink especially with heating pipes running underneath them. To avoid excessive gaps, buy wood wide enough to fit tightly.

Butt-jointed It is unlikely that old boards will match new sizes of planed timber. Planed timber described as 150mm × 25mm (6 in × 1 in) PAR is actually finished smaller usually by 3mm (⅛ in). Such a small measurement is not a problem on the odd board, but if there are two or three together the gap is significant and can show through a carpet and underlay.

It might be possible to spread the gap over the boards or even put an in-fill strip down one edge. If the boards are to be seen, the only way to solve the problem is to have them cut to size or if you have a power saw, run them down yourself from a larger size of timber.

Tongued and grooved Tongued and grooved (T&G) boards will be impossible to replace with all the interlocking sections, but on short lengths this is not really too important.

If the old boards are good enough to reuse, trim the ragged edges with a plane or surform and place them as butt-jointed boards.

Boards that are too badly damaged must be replaced with new T&G. Interlock as many edges as you can.

Chipboard flooring This is becoming the normal material for flooring, not because it is more suitable, but because it is cheaper than wood. Chipboard is fixed in large sheets with tongued and grooved edges. Once a sheet has been cut and lifted it must not be put back with the edges unsupported.

To support the edges use 100mm × 50mm (4 in × 2 in) lengths of timber cut in between the joists. Cut with a very slight taper so they will partly support themselves, but still use a nail or two at each end.

Supporting ends All the board ends must be supported, preferably over joists, but never by the pipes running underneath.

If the board is cut short of the joist, use a packing piece or 'L'-shaped brackets to support the floating edge. Support boards midway over joists where possible – if not, use supports. Edges of chipboard sheets can be supported with steel banding strip laid across the joists and nailed.

Stagger joints alternately over joists so that all the boards do not end on the same joist, thereby creating a weak spot.

'DO NOT NAIL'
Do not rely on your memory when fixing down boards. Use a felt-tip pen to mark, on top of the boards, the position of pipes and cables, and write 'Do not nail' on vulnerable points.

Screw down the ends with No. 12 64-mm (2½-in) countersunk wood screws threaded all the way up to help prevent any future movement.

Hardboard

If the floorboards do not go back well enough to hide the bumps and gaps, you can lay hardboard over the entire area. As well as keeping down draughts, it forms an ideal surface for vinyl sheet and tiles and can also be carpeted over. Dampen the sheets of hardboard first to swell them slightly so they shrink when fixed, and then lay them flat.

Staple or nail the hardboard to the floorboards, with the nails driven well home at 150-mm (6-in) intervals.

When refixing screw down rather than nail floorboards to prevent squeaking.

Hardboard should be pinned at 150mm centres to prevent it floating.

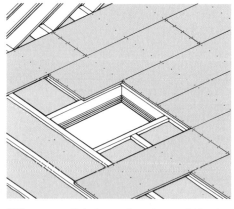

Where possible keep the pipes within the insulated area of the building. Stagger the ends of boards over joists.

GLOSSARY

Actuator
Electrically powered motor section of motorized valve.

Air cock
Valve for allowing air to be released from a heating system.

Annealing
Removing hardness in a metal by heat-treatment to make it more workable.

Ball valve or ballcock
An automatic float-operated valve used to control the water level in tanks and wc cisterns.

Bib cock
Angled tap for screwing into wall-mounted backplate inlet.

Blanking plate, blanking plug
A threaded plug for capping the immersion heater boss on a hot water cylinder if no heater is fitted.

Bore
Internal dimension of pipe.

Boss
A threaded hole in a hot water cylinder in which an immersion heater is fitted.

Capillary joint
Soldered joint in which the solder is drawn between the fitting and the pipe by capillary action.

Check valve
One-way valve that prevents flow back into the supply pipe in the event of a drop in water pressure.

Combination boiler
A boiler that combines central heating and hot water inside its casing and needs no tanks or cylinders.

Compression joint
Mechanical joint in which a metal ring or olive is compressed on to the pipe to form a seal between it and the fitting.

Cylinder coil
A copper heat-exchanging coil found inside an indirect cylinder.

Dip pipe
An extension to the overflow pipe inside a cold-water storage cistern that ends just below the filled water level and prevents back-draughts that could cause freezing.

Diverter valve
Manually or electrically controlled valve used to switch flow from one circuit to another.

Draincock
Key- or spanner-operated valve with a hosepipe connector that allows a heating system to be drained.

Essex flange
A device which enables a pipe to be connected to a hot water cylinder where no tapped union exists.

Expansion vessel
Container to catch excess water caused by expansion on heating in a direct hot-water system.

Facia, fascia
Board fixed to the outer ends of rafters to which the brackets for supporting guttering are attached.

Feed
Water supply pipe.

Feed and expansion tank
Central heating tank used to supply water for radiators and boiler and also to accommodate extra volume of water which occurs during heating.

Flaunching
Mortar layer for sealing a chimney pot or flue terminal to the stack.

Flexi-connector
Softened or corrugated copper pipe connectors that are easily bent to join taps to existing pipework.

Flue, balanced
Boiler terminal that admits the correct quantity of air for combustion as well as passing out the waste gases.

Flue, conventional
Vertical pipe for combustion gases that relies on the updraught of the hot gases to draw them safely away.

Flow pressure regulator
A spring-loaded valve used to maintain a constant pressure and flow rate through a circuit.

Flux
Paste used in soldering to prevent oxidisation of metal before solder has run.

Gate valve
Screw-down valve in which a metal plate is lowered to stop the flow. Used in low-pressure parts of a water system.

Gland
A seal in taps and stop valves to prevent water from leaking out through the mechanism.

Gravity circulation
Circulation of water in a heating system caused by hot water rising and cooler water falling because of the lower density of the hot water.

Grommet
A washer fitted between the backnut and socket of a connector to form a watertight seal.

Head
Water pressure created by the height of a water storage tank above an outlet tap or shower.

Header tank
See Feed and expansion tank.

Heat exchanger
Portion of a boiler in which heat from the burners is transferred to the water in the heating system.

In line connectors
Well-insulated water-resistant push fit electrical connectors for joining two flexes together.

Jumper plate
Brass plate for holding tap washer.

Lockshield valve
Radiator valve at the other end to the on/off valve, for balancing the water flow to give equal heating to all the radiators.

MDPE
Medium density polyethylene. Plastic pipe used mainly for underground supplies.

Motorized valve
Electrically powered control valves wired into thermostats to control hot water and central heating temperatures.

Non return valve
Spring-loaded one way valve used to prevent back flow or siphonage of possibly contaminated water into drinking supplies.

O-ring
Circular section rubber ring that forms a seal around a tap spindle or between a pipe and a push-fit joint.

Portsmouth valve
Ballvalve design now superceded by new British standard pattern, but still commonly found in many homes.

Pressure valve
Valve activated by pressure either as a safety release or as a switch.

PTFE
Polytetrafluoroethylene. Water and heat resistant sealing compound used as sealing tape on threaded joints.

Push fit
A rubber seal ring fitting into which a pipe is inserted. This fitting cannot be tightened.

RCD
An electrical safety circuit breaker which measures the current and switches off if there is any imbalance.

Self-tapping connectors
Clamp-on connectors for supply and waste pipes that cut into the existing pipe and are self-sealing.

Service pipe
Underground pipe connecting the water main to the internal (consumer) stopcock.

Service valve
Isolating valve fitted in the supply pipe to an appliance for ease of servicing.

Shroud
Cosmetic cover that conceals a tap mechanism.

Single stack system
A modern soil and waste system which uses one vertical pipe for used wc and washing waste pipes.

Slip-tee valve
Valve having no pipe stop on one of its compression fittings to allow it to be slid along a cut pipe for ease of connection.

Solenoid valve
Electrically-operated valve in which the valve is opened and closed by an electro-magnet.

Spigot
Plain end of pipe on to which another is pushed. Usually drainage.

Standpipe
Vertical waste pipe into which a washing machine or dishwasher outlet hose can be hooked for connection to the waste system.

Stillson
Adjustable plumber's wrench with toothed jaws for gripping pipes.

Stink pipe
A popular name for a drainage vent pipe.

Stopcock
Control valve normally used to turn off cold water mains.

Supa taps
Patented design of taps which allows rewashering without turning off the water supplies.

Tails
The threaded portion below a tap to which the supply pipe is joined via a tap connector.

Tapping
Threaded union to which pipe connections are made.

Thermostat
Automatic temperature-operated switch.

TRV
Abbreviation for thermostatic radiator valve – one which can be set to open and close at a certain air temperature.

Unvented cylinder
A new type of cylinder in the UK which has a pressure vessel and safety valve and is fed directly from the mains water supply.

Union
Brass-faced threaded joint in two parts for joining pipes and fittings.

Vent pipe
A pipe open to the atmosphere to provide an escape route for overheated water from a cylinder. Also the top section of a soil pipe or waste pipe which provides air to the drains.

Zone valve
Motorized or solenoid control valve used to open and close flow to one circuit.

INDEX